# SET FOR LIFE

How to Create Happiness
in a Way Too Busy World

## ED ELGARRESTA

PUBLISHED BY

A NONFICTION IMPRINT FROM ADDUCENT

ADDUCENT, INC.
WWW.ADDUCENTINC.COM
TITLES DISTRIBUTED IN

North America
United Kingdom
Western Europe
South America
Australia
China
India

# Set For Life

How to Create Happiness in a Way Too Busy World

Ed Elgarresta

Copyright © 2016. All rights reserved. No part of this book may be reproduced or transmitted in any form or by any means, electronic or mechanical, including photocopying, recording or by any information storage and retrieval system, without written permission from the author, except for brief quotations as would be used in a review.

ISBN 9781937592653 (paperback)

Published by INSPIRE, an imprint from Adducent

www.AdducentInc.com

All statements of fact, opinion, or analysis expressed are those of the author and do not reflect the official positions or views of the publisher. Nothing in the contents should be construed as asserting and or implying authentication of information or endorsement of the author's views. This book and subjects discussed within are designed to provide the author's opinion about the subject matter covered and is for informational purposes only.

# TABLE OF CONTENTS

**Dedication & Acknowledgments**
**Preface:** *What Did You Expect (Out of Life)?*   1
**Introducing Set For Life Planning**   15
   *What SFL Planning Is and Is Not*   15
   *How This Book is Organized*   20
   *Making the Three Pillars Part of Your Life*   23
   *Who Can Benefit from this Book?*   24
   *The Promise*   26
**Using Your Brain's Wiring to Create a More Exciting Life**   29
   *Why Material Possessions May Not Make You Happy*   30
   *Risk, Reward and Evolution*   31
**A Walk Down Memory Lane**   36
   *The Importance of Memories in our Lives*   36
   *The Different Types of Memories*   38
**Why Is It So Hard to Stay Happy?**   48
   *Not Depressed? Great! But are You Happy?*   51
   *Creating Intentional Happiness*   56
**Living Life with Zest**   60
   *Adding Emotion to Help Achieve Goals*   62
**Set For Life Pillars**   66
   *Pillar 1: Experiences*   67
   *Pillar 2: Anticipation*   90
   *Pillar 3: Choices*   105
**Set For Life in Action**   125
   *Making It Real*   126

## Making SFL Planning Part of Your Life
143
*The Planning System* 144
*Writing Your Life Story* 155
*Living Your Life Story* 163
## Conclusion
170
## References
175
## Resources
179
## About the Author
180

# DEDICATION & ACKNOWLEDGMENTS

To my family, my wife, Christina, and my children, Katy and Tommy, who I love and adore immeasurably. This is for them. Without them and my desire to bring them the joy and memories they deserve, the idea for this book would have never been born. Often times I needed a powerful and inspiring reason to keep going. You were it.

To my parents, my mother who always supported me and my biggest cheerleader. Everyone should be so lucky to have someone like her by their side. Her wisdom is as deep as it is endless. My father who taught me to enjoy life, now. He showed me the importance of perspective and to have fun in this journey called life. And my siblings who I love being around. I am blessed to be surrounded by the most powerful force there is, unconditional love.

To my sounding board, Dennis Lowery who not only validated my thinking, but contributed significantly to the finished book. I enjoyed exchanging *Set For Life* stories with you. Working with you made for a wonderful experience and memory.

Thank you, Madelyn Stone, for refining, polishing, and giving me an English lesson along the way. Your editing was superb. Your ideas thoughtful.

Finally, there have been many other family members, friends, and co-workers who have been part of my life. You have helped shaped me as a person and as a professional. The experiences I have had along the way with you have contributed to the *Set For Life* approach. One cannot live and not be shaped by all who come into our lives.

# PREFACE
## What Did You Expect (Out of Life)?

*"It's never too late to have a happy childhood."*

-- Tom Robbins

If you are like most ambitious people, you started your adult life with an expectation of what your life was going to be like, and more specifically, with the expectation of the type of lifestyle you were going to live. You were going to make a difference in the lives of others, or you were going to enjoy a life of discovery and adventure. Perhaps you had hopes for a family life filled with love, closeness, and joy. These personal beliefs are real and genuine.

Maybe you had the foresight to think about how your career was going to fuel your desired lifestyle, and so you had a vision of what was to be. Perhaps you had a lofty outlook for your career. Your ambition and go-get-it attitude were going to fuel your rise through the ranks of corporate America, or perhaps your sense of independence was going to enable and empower your entrepreneurial spirit.

Whether your dreams were big or small, like most people, you expected that life was going to lead you to a greater, more exciting and fulfilling place—you were on a journey to a happy life. But then life happened, and you stepped right into it.

## WHAT YOU HOPED FOR, BUT...

For many years, those expectations and desires are alive and vibrant, both personally and professionally. It isn't until ten, twenty, and sometimes thirty years later that something clicks inside and a feeling of disillusionment begins to surface. If it happens early on in life and continues unabated and unaddressed, frustration creeps in and likely increases to intolerable levels.

Regrets and remorse set in with the realization that your life dreams have been marginalized into prioritized to-do lists and deadlines. The reality of the daily grind—the bills, home maintenance, and work commitments—also sets in. Somewhere along the way, the illusion of living a *Leave It to Beaver* family life is also betrayed by the actuality of being a parent in today's society. All the daily demands of being a mother or father—the eat-your-breakfast and bathtime wars, the seemingly endless homework projects, social media vigilance, and unyielding after-school and weekend activities—prevail.

And so, the days, weeks, months, and years go by.

The outlook for a work–life balance also

changes. The sheer requirements to be successful in your career are greater than you originally thought. And the increasing responsibilities come fast with the added pressure of speed and performance. Though you are still ambitious and continue to strive for success, your career certainly takes up much more time than you had expected. In unanticipated ways, your success and ambition encroach on your personal life expectations. And that is okay while you are still getting established and gaining much-needed experience, making a name for yourself and building a positive reputation.

If you are one of the fortunate ones, you enjoy your career. After all, it is honorable to earn a living that can afford a lifestyle of your choice. But many people, after years of sacrifice, are never quite able to reach that point where they feel they have "made it." Their lives are not at a stage where they feel they have accomplished what they dreamed about years ago as young men and women. In fact, it isn't that way at all. With each passing year, it is one more promotion, one more "exciting" job assignment, or one more job change. "This time," they tell themselves, "with the right job, I will have it all, and I will be happy." But that next promotion, new assignment, or new job never comes, or worse yet, it does, but it never quite gives them the peace of mind and happiness they fought for and dreamed of for so long. And so, despite the hard work and diligently marking off the To-Dos that is supposed to lead to success, they're not as happy as they thought they'd be.

Sound familiar? It was this way for me. I believe it is still this way for many ambitious, success-driven people.

So, many who have carefully planned their lives and accomplished their goals are still not as happy or as fulfilled as they thought they'd be. And what about those who have led lives not as well thought out—those who react to and passively accept their circumstances? In some cosmic irony, they, too, have reached self-awareness of self-inflicted frustration—they shot low and hit the mark. But they, too, can't shake the feeling that they could be happier. If only they knew what to do.

## WHAT THEY DON'T TEACH IN SCHOOL (BUT SHOULD)

In school, they teach the physical makeup of the brain in science classes; they'll even touch upon the functions of the different parts, but there's very little, if any, discussion on what physically happens in the brain at its most basic level to make us feel happy and content. And yet, knowing this can significantly affect our lives.

What we think, what we do, how we respond and react to our circumstances, largely determine how our lives unfold.

Most of us have to figure out through trial and error – if we do at all, why we think the way we do and what that means.

Only a rare few of us study (or understand) how to use our brains or what happens in our brains—what our brains actually "do"—to create positive and happy feelings.

And, most importantly, few of us understand how we can use our minds to our advantage and plan in a way that leads to happier, more contented lives.

How we use our heads works to shape our experiences and create memories that are important to whom we become, how happy we are and how our lives turn out.

This is not a subject commonly covered in school: certainly, not in grades one through twelve or even early (if ever) in college. But it should be.

Whether your life is going according to your plan but you are still not as fulfilled as you envisioned or if your life 'just happened,' and where you are, is where you just came to be. Rest assured, you are now on your way to leading a more exciting and fulfilling life, one of meaningful memories and experiences you actively create. The *Set For Life* planning principles and system described in this book will help you design and live a life you will enjoy and look forward to remembering.

## YOU ARE YOUR MEMORIES

*"Memory is the diary that we all carry about with us."*
--Oscar Wilde

Your memory—and your *memories* in particular—make up the glue that binds your life. Memory is the foundation of how we learn to eat, walk, and talk. We use it when we recall the happy and sad times with our families and friends. Whether we are reliving our high school days during class reunions or rehashing old Thanksgiving Day stories about our favorite uncle, our memories are central to it all. Memories are how we know what's right or wrong for us; they tell us what we prefer and enjoy—and what we don't. They shape all facets of our personality. They also influence how we behave when faced with certain circumstances.

*The memories we make throughout our lives are of the utmost importance.* This point needs to be emphasized. Each one of us has a unique past and present that becomes the pages and chapters of our life stories. This unique past and present also sets the stage for an unwritten future that will hopefully become a wonderful story with us as the main character. Past, present, and future memories—all the memories you have now and those you create today and tomorrow—truly matter in the quality of your life.

We have neglected the importance to the quality of our lives of making positive memories. We have been so focused on leading "productive" lives we have ignored, never learned or have never understood that the *memories* we make with family, friends, and our communities are what ultimately increase our happiness. The *Set For Life Planning System (SFL)* introduced in this book changes this and enables you to design and live a life you will look forward to remembering.

## The Life You Live

*"No man on his deathbed ever looked up into the eyes of his family and friends and said, 'I wish I'd spent more time at the office.'"*

--John Piper

We've all heard that quote or some variation of it many times throughout our lives. We are so compelled by a drive within us to excel and rise to the top that we ignore, or at least disregard, its importance. Instead, we focus on getting ourselves into better jobs or push to get the next promotion. Call it the "puritanical work ethic" we inherited or an innate drive for a desired level of achievement. Either way, we are driven to accomplish short-term goals but often forget to put the diverse dimensions of our lives into long-term perspective.

The question many of us struggle to answer is whether we are equipped to fully interweave the personal and career aspects of our lives in ways that complement rather than compete with each other. We live in a frenetic, overly busy time; we are expected to do more, lots more, with the same twenty-four hours we've always had and always will have. And to make things more challenging, technology and the Internet have amped up the speed and expectations of deadlines. Connected at all times, our smartphones and mobile devices are excellent for reminding us of meetings and of all of our tasks. Being linked that way not only leads to multitasking, but also makes it too easy to switch between the personal and professional roles we play. We end up unable to be "in the present," "in the moment," in a single role, and it is usually our loved ones and our personal relationships that suffer the consequences.

## Did You Know?

> The average person checks their phone 150 times a day! The average time we work on a task before being interrupted? Just one minute and 15 seconds. So, it's not surprising that research from Stanford University found that multitasking is less productive than doing a single thing at a time. And want to feel like an 8-year old again? A study at the University of London found

that participants who multitasked during cognitive tasks experienced IQ score declines that were similar to what they'd expect if they had smoked marijuana. IQ drops of 15 points for multitasking men lowered their scores to the average range of an 8-year-old child.

## PRODUCTIVITY DOES NOT EQUATE TO HAPPINESS

As a society, we are obsessed with productivity and getting more done in less time. And some would argue that's fitting given our desired lifestyles and ambitions. The less time it takes us to get things done, the more time we have for leisure, for spending with our families and friends, and for doing what we want to do. It's hard to argue against that logic. That model works if you have discrete work that can be turned on and off. But what if the flow of work from both your career and personal activities, all of which need to be done, is continuous? What happens when work and life become even more tightly intertwined than they are now? Or, what if you choose to devote more time to your career during certain phases of your life, such as just before an opportunity for a promotion? While people are typically hyperproductive during these points in their careers, does it need to be at the expense of happiness and satisfaction in the other parts of their lives? And what of those individuals who are born alpha-type go-getters, enterprising people raised with a punishing work ethic and even stronger drive. Are these people on the path to less-than-fulfilling and unhappy lives? Perhaps. Perhaps not.

## WHAT DO YOU REMEMBER?

We often resort to managing our lives—personal and professional—with lists just to help us prioritize and keep us on task to get through the day. But if you were to recall last week, what would you remember? Would it be the minutiae? Would it be the lists you made and items you checked or didn't check off? What is it that stands out from your everyday activities? Stop for a moment and think about what specific memories you have from last week, last month, or last year that would be worth sharing with a family member or dear friend.

The reality is we often don't stop for a moment and think about the life we are leading. There's just not enough time (so we think) to sit down and consider whether a more fulfilling life exists or is even possible. In other words:

Can we be happier given our current circumstances? What do we need to do to make that happen?

We are so busy navigating through the here and now that we don't take the time to reflect on the life story we're writing every day. More importantly, we don't even take the time to think about the life story we *want* to create. And yet, at the end of our lives, memories are all we have to look back on.

So, a question we should ask ourselves is whether the memories we have—both in quality and quantity—are of completed or incomplete checklists or of exciting and meaningful experiences.

I decided to take a hard look at how successful I was at living my own life and asked that very question not many years ago. I was (and am) professionally successful. I also have a loving wife and two beautiful children. For all intents and purposes, I was successful. But in the end, it came down to whether my reality was meeting my expectations for the entirety of my life. I thought there could be, and I desired, more in different areas of my life. It was at that point that I needed to figure out whether my expectations were too high (I hoped not), or whether I needed to give up some things from a career and/or family life standpoint to improve my overall well-being. I didn't like that option, either.

There were several key ideas I had learned from my career experiences and from my own personal development. They were—and are—what I found missing from the various life planning and time management strategies available at the time and even today. They filled the information void and are covered in the following pages. Many of these concepts are based on the research and findings from the experts, scientists, and researchers who spend their days studying what makes people happy—and what does not. For the ambitious professional and those who just feel busy all the time, there are relevant research findings on what to incorporate into our busy lives that can increase our overall happiness. That science and research, proven in the real world are at the core of what I'm going to tell you about, and why it works.

## DID YOU KNOW?

A palliative nurse who has counseled the dying in their last days has revealed the most common regrets we have at the end of our lives.

Bronnie Ware is an Australian nurse who spent several years working in palliative care, caring for patients in the last 12 weeks of their lives. She recorded their dying epiphanies in a blog called Inspiration and Chai, which gathered so much attention that she put her observations into a book called "The Top Five Regrets of the Dying." Ware writes of the phenomenal clarity of vision that people gain at the end of their lives, and how we might learn from their wisdom. "When questioned about any regrets they had or anything they would do differently," she says, "common themes surfaced again and again."

Here are the top five regrets of the dying, as witnessed by Ware:

1. I wish I'd had the courage to live a life true to myself, not the life others expected of me. "This was the most common regret of all. When people realize that their life is almost over and look back clearly on it, it is easy to see how many dreams have gone unfulfilled. Most people had not honored even a half of their dreams and had to die knowing that it was due to choices they had made, or not made. Health brings a freedom very few realize, until they no longer have it."
2. I wish I hadn't worked so hard. "This came from every male patient that I nursed. They missed their children's youth and their partner's companionship. Women also spoke of this regret, but as most were from an older generation, many of the female patients had not been breadwinners. All of the men I nursed deeply regretted spending so much of their lives on the treadmill of a work existence."
3. I wish I'd had the courage to express my feelings. "Many people suppressed their feelings in order to keep peace with others. As a result, they settled for a mediocre existence and never became who they were truly capable of becoming. Many developed illnesses relating to the bitterness and resentment they carried as a result."
4. I wish I had stayed in touch with my friends. "Often they would not truly realize the full benefits of old friends until their dying weeks and it was not always possible to track them down. Many had become so caught up in their own lives that they had let golden friendships slip by over the years. There were many deep regrets about not giving friendships the time

and effort that they deserved. Everyone misses their friends when they are dying."

5. I wish that I had let myself be happier. "This is a surprisingly common one. Many did not realize until the end that happiness is a choice. They had stayed stuck in old patterns and habits. The so-called 'comfort' of familiarity overflowed into their emotions, as well as their physical lives. Fear of change had them pretending to others, and to their selves, that they were content, when deep within, they longed to laugh properly and have silliness in their life again."

# INTRODUCING SET FOR LIFE (SFL) PLANNING

*"The purpose of life is to live it, to taste experience to the utmost, to reach out eagerly and without fear for newer and richer experience."*

--Eleanor Roosevelt

## WHAT SFL PLANNING IS

There have been many advances and discoveries in the areas of happiness and on living a fulfilling life. Yet checklists and task management have persisted to dominate our planning options. Increasing our productivity continues to be the focus while we disregard what truly makes life exciting and memorable. We know through research that experiences affect happiness and overall well-being. The *SFL Planning* approach reinforces and supports the intentional planning of experiences and activities that increase happiness. There is no other planning system like it, nothing similar to what you are about to learn.

The *SFL Planning* core principle is that *actively*

*and thoughtfully planning certain types of experiences in the areas of your life that are most important to you will lead to increased personal happiness and meaning.* The *SFL Planning* approach applies this principle and gives you the strategies you need to do more of the things you enjoy and want to do to add more meaning and excitement in your life.

*SFL Planning* relies on life experiences and making memories as the central drivers to accomplish those strategies. *SFL Planning* incorporates what has been found from research studies to be important contributors to a person's happiness. While most other planning systems focus on either productivity or scheduling, *SFL Planning* approaches it from a different angle; it is based on research on how your brain works and what you can specifically do to increase your happiness levels.

*SFL Planning* also emphasizes the importance of contextual planning. Life situations and experiences differ and evolve based on what phase of life you are in and what's important at that point. That's the context of your life, and simply put, life changes. You play different roles, or desire to play different roles, depending on what's happening in your life at that time. The *SFL* approach to planning will help guide you to identify those roles that matter most and how to actively create an exciting and compelling future for them. The experiences you live are unique to you and have meaning within the setting of your life. It's time to design a life story that will make you the happiest while also helping you make more meaningful contributions to the lives of those around you.

*SFL Planning* is effective in that it marries key strategies with an action-oriented framework so you can put it to work quickly and easily. It includes the processes to support and enable this new way of thinking and planning. The *SFL Planning* concepts can complement your existing planning approach, or it can be a stand-alone, all-inclusive framework structured to allow you to plan an experience-filled and memorable life.

## WHAT SFL PLANNING IS NOT

The topic of planning and productivity is widely discussed and written about. It's best to compare and contrast more traditional planning tools and techniques with the *SFL Planning* approach and see how it is different. While valuable, you will *not* find the following topics contained in the *SFL* approach:

1. We're *not* going to talk about the best time of day you should work on your most important projects.
2. We're *not* going to discuss how you should structure your day.
3. We're *not* going to review task management

workflows.
4. And we're *not* going to discuss the merits of particular prioritization methods.

These and many other similar concepts have been covered effectively in other books and strategies. They are primarily focused on making you more efficient and saving time. These are significant and valuable, and I have personally benefited from many productivity techniques. However, they do not, in and of themselves, lead you to long-term happiness or a more fulfilling and meaningful life.

*SFL Planning* is *not*, at its core, a traditional time management or planning tool. There is no doubt we can all benefit from being more efficient, better organized, and getting more things done in a day. Some good books out there will help you in those areas. This book, candidly, is not one of them.

As long as we're on the topic of organization, let me comment on lists. I know many list makers. I'm one of them. I'm a big believer in lists of all kinds: To-Do lists, shopping lists, reminder lists, and tickler files. I keep them digitally (Smartphone, laptop, and tablet), and I also use paper-based lists (index cards are my favorite). But I know that remembering what to buy at the grocery store or having a reminder for when to make a phone call does not lead to long-term happiness. Looking for joy and fulfillment in a checklist is a fool's journey. Being efficient may be satisfying and give you peace of mind, but it's not going to create the stories and memories you can look back upon and cherish ten years from now.

When was the last time you had a grand old time sharing your checklist with your friends? If you can recall such an occurrence—please stop and reread from the beginning—we have a lot of work to do on you!

The system behind *SFL Planning* is not intended to make you more organized. In the working world, increasing productivity and efficiencies are common goals in most companies' strategic plans and are admirable personal goals as well. Leading organizations often make increasing efficiencies and reaping the associated cost savings a top priority. Companies, and the people who work for them, can certainly benefit from being more productive and efficient. However, in the end, companies only survive and thrive because they continue to evolve and grow and remain relevant to their customers.

Likewise, while individuals may search for ways to become more productive, it will not foster personal growth or happiness. They need to seek and create those experiences that will create growth, meaning, and happiness in their lives.

Is it one or the other? Is it a competition only one will win: productivity versus happiness? Of course, not; they can, and ideally should, coexist. *SFL Planning* incorporates many principles which are complementary to any productivity and time management method you may already have in place. In many ways, it enhances the productivity gains you receive from other time management tools as you pursue the things that matter most for your quality of life.

## How This Book Is Organized

The book is organized to first provide you an overview of how the *SFL Planning* approach aligns and leverages how our brains are wired to increase our happiness. I'll go through some important mechanisms in our brains that we influence with *SFL Planning* and are the basis for why this approach is effective in increasing our happiness levels.

Then the key *SFL Planning* concepts, which I call "Pillars," will be reviewed and will be followed by examples of *SFL Planning* in action so you get a sense of how it plays out in real life.

Finally, a more detailed look at a question-driven process you can use to put the *SFL Planning System* to work in your life is presented.

Knowing the ideas and concepts you want to improve is the easy part. The difficult, more challenging part is trying to put them into practice. The reality is that change is hard...very hard. It doesn't matter if you've just bought a new smartphone, are learning to use it, or have a new briefcase and are figuring out which pockets to put all the stuff in from the old one. Change is inherently difficult for people; so, I've highlighted ideas and helpful tips in the section covering the *SFL Planning System* that helped me make it easier to apply.

If you are already using a planning system, you may find that you want to incorporate one or some of the key *SFL* concepts into your existing process. Go with what works for you. It's not an all-or-nothing model; in fact, you may prefer to implement selected concepts incrementally rather than all at once. This will allow you to judge what works and what doesn't as you add more layers to your planning process.

## INTRODUCING THE THREE PILLARS OF SFL PLANNING

While I will go over the three pillars of the *SFL Planning* approach in more detail later in the book, I do want to introduce them to you now so you get a sense of what to expect. Each of the pillars are important, but when you put them together they can be life changing.

## Pillar 1: Purposely Plan and Create Experiences into Your Life

*Experiential Planning* is a foundational concept for *SFL Planning*. Experiences, rather than mere goals, are deeper and more meaningful because they are linked to emotions. The experiences you plan will help you create meaningful memories you will remember and want to share with others. However, not all experiences are created equal. This book describes what an *SFL Experience* is and why it leads to increased levels of happiness in your life.

## Pillar 2: Plan Anticipation into Your Life

We often look forward to events, vacations, and special occasions, but we don't typically intentionally plan specific activities that increasingly build our level of excitement. We expand and enrich our overall experience to make it even more memorable and meaningful by planning in related events and activities that create anticipation.

## Pillar 3: Make Choices to Focus on What Matters Most

Taking an active approach to identifying and developing the most important roles you play in your life will enable you to lead and experience a life full of happiness and excitement in the areas of your life that matter most. Either you focus on, and intentionally create, the opportunities to shape your future or someone else will do it for you. Sitting passively on the sidelines is safe, but it's also a potential dead-end of disappointment and regrets.

## MAKING THE THREE PILLARS PART OF YOUR LIFE

New strategies and new ways of doing something are only good if you actually put them to use for your benefit. Too often, we read or hear about concepts that sound great only to find we ignore or forget to use them in our daily lives. Productivity books are notorious for this: great-sounding ideas and top ten tips that simply are not practical in a person's life or are challenging to implement.

The issue is how to incorporate the *SFL* ideas into your every day activities. In other words, how do you use what you learned right away and within the context of your life and make it part of a routine? Without the explicit knowledge, process, and tools to put the concepts into practice, you inevitably fail.

The *SFL Planning System* described in this book has incorporated the fundamental *SFL* concepts into a question-based planning process to make it a part of your everyday life - easily and quickly.

## WHO CAN BENEFIT FROM THIS BOOK?

*SFL Planning* was designed, above all, for people who have—whether by choice or not—a career and personal life that aren't well balanced. Their existence is often more career than life. And they are very busy. *SFL Planning* provides an approach so they don't have to compromise on their professional ambitions. It works regardless of what career or what phase of life you are in. There are particular types of actions to take that will create the kind of experiences and memories you will remember and cherish and also establish that balance you seek – even if just balanced in your own mind. While *SFL Planning* is effective for anyone, these targeted strategies are especially helpful for ambitious professionals who do not want to abandon their career goals but who also want to add new dimensions, excitement, and happiness to their lives. This book is particularly relevant to those who:

1. Live day by day, taking things as they come. Planning your personal life is ad hoc, if at all. You live in a perpetual state of rush-rush and often wake up or feel you are in a state of "OMG, I'm-already-late." You are more reactionary than proactive.
2. Go for a week, a month, or even a year and wonder

what you've done that was meaningful. Or worse, you don't even wonder at all.
3. Don't typically plan and look forward to an event, such as a vacation, a date night, time with your loved ones, and so on. Instead, things happen to you…they don't happen through your actions.
4. Live a highly predictable and mundane life.
5. Feel like you barely coexist with your family and wonder if there is something more you could be doing.

*SFL Planning* specifically aims to increase your happiness and satisfaction with your life. The principles and tools behind *SFL Planning* will empower you to create a life full of memorable experiences, the type you will look back on and cherish. Though these strategies are best learned early—if you are a parent or mentor, please pass on what you're about to learn to the young people in your life—these lessons are never too late to adopt for adults of any age. *SFL Planning* is multidimensional and can be tailored to your situation and life. Using the *SFL Planning* strategies, you come to understand, appreciate, and focus on the areas in your life that matter most and doing the things which contribute to making you and those you care most about happy.

No one but you can create your life. You have the ability to make it memorable, happy, and fulfilling.

Similarly, you are fully capable of creating one that is unremarkable. Which one will you choose? Are you happy with where you are today; could you be happier? Are you living a truly fulfilling life in the areas most important to you? If not, read on.

## THE PROMISE

What you will find in the following pages is a system that can significantly increase your personal fulfillment and enjoyment in life. You can use the *SFL Planning* strategies to enhance your existing approach to life planning, or you can use its broader end-to-end method to help you become more fruitful in the areas that should matter most.

As in any personal planning system, it needs to work for you within the context of your current personal situation. Your life is dynamic and changes year to year, probably even more frequently. You can be single and carefree one year, and married with a child the next. Our lives change and we need to deal with those changes. As you move through the stages of your life, your approach to planning may need to adapt. A planning system outlives its usefulness when you find yourself spending more time fitting your life into it than the other way around. That's when that planning system becomes extinct.

I have tried many planning systems, and some

worked for a while. But then my situation changed and my goals would get disconnected from my planning. I had a hard time integrating new or longer-term goals into my everyday planning. The systems I used ultimately became nothing more than "next action" checklists. They served me well from a task management standpoint, but there was something missing—something larger and more meaningful. I needed something more that worked based on how real life is lived. It had to be flexible and adaptive. It had to change when my life changed, when my goals changed. And I wanted it to support a planning process that enabled me to write the pages and chapters of an exciting and fulfilling life story. I promise you will find that in this book.

**Important Points to Remember**

1. Life happens, whether we plan it or not.
2. If we aren't as happy as we thought we'd be, we can change that.
3. Purposely planning and living memorable experiences are key ingredients to a happier life.
4. Happiness is tied to the right kind of experiences—the ones that create positive memories—and not to being more "productive."
5. The *SFL* Planning strategies work for the busy and ambitious professionals who want to add new dimensions and excitement to their lives.

6. The *SFL Planning* philosophy, principles, and system are intended to be flexible to support any phase of life you are in.

# USING YOUR BRAIN'S WIRING TO CREATE A MORE EXCITING LIFE

*"Memory is assisted by anything that makes an impression on a powerful passion, inspiring fear, for example, or wonder, shame, or joy."*

--Francis Bacon

In this book, you will read about the importance of experiences in your life and the positive impact experiences can have on the quality of your life.

But before we get into that, it's important to learn something about how your amazing brain works. You can then get an appreciation for why *SFL Planning* is effective and how to use this knowledge to approach planning in a fresh way to add more zest, fun, and excitement to your life.

Having a life plan that works instead of a life without a plan, or a poorly conceived one, will put the odds of living a happy and memorable life in your favor.

We've all heard how material possessions don't make you happy or some variation of this, such as money doesn't buy you happiness. And, for the most part, this is true. Studies have shown that once our basic needs of survival and comfort are met, incremental money over and above that amount does not have a significant effect on our happiness.

## WHY MATERIAL POSSESSIONS MAY NOT MAKE YOU HAPPY

Now, having read that, you might have just muttered something like, "Did I just purchase a book that tells me money won't buy me happiness? Please, please, please, don't tell me I spent my money on this advice." Well, you did, partly, but it doesn't end there. There is more to this—much more. We all know having money in itself doesn't guarantee happiness. Research has shown us that having a lot of possessions won't result in long-term happiness. Perhaps you know people, too, who have plenty of everything but never seem truly happy. But—and it's a big BUT—research is showing us that having certain types of experiences, even if you do purchase them, can lead to increased levels of happiness in your life. And the research points us to the specific types of activities and experiences that result in positive feelings. (There is more on this to come.) So, it's not just enough to say money doesn't buy you happiness. And it's not sufficient to say having experiences will increase your happiness level—although it is a start. It's planning and having the right type of experiences as part of your life that will increase your well-being and give you a sense of satisfaction. You may be asking, but why is this true? To answer that question, we have to look at where we came from.

## RISK, REWARD, AND EVOLUTION

### Partnering with Your Caveman Brain

Humans evolved from a very scary place, a place where they didn't know when they went hunting whether they would catch lunch or be lunch. Back in the old caveman days, our ancestral family was surrounded by aggressive and hungry animals. It was a violent world.

Survival of the fittest was the mantra for primitive man and woman. Fortunately for all subsequent humans, the brain of our caveman ancestor–let's call him Dennis–evolved to a point where survival—and the survival of his fellow Cro-Magnons—was very high on his priority to-do list. And I say evolved because after enough time—a really long time—the human body developed a mechanism that was fueled by tiny chemicals called *neurotransmitters*. These chemicals drive much, if not all, of our behavior, our thinking, our remembering, and our actions. Neurotransmitters are the brain chemicals that communicate information throughout our mind and body. They relay signals between nerve cells, called neurons. The brain uses them to tell your heart to beat, your lungs to breathe, and your stomach to digest. They influence your personality, too. They are involved in every part of every function in your body. They can also affect mood, sleep, concentration, weight, and can cause adverse symptoms when they are out of balance, which is not uncommon as an estimated 86 percent of Americans have suboptimal neurotransmitter levels. Needless to say, neurotransmitters are an essential part to who we are. And why is this important to us as it relates to *SFL Planning*?

Because they also trigger happiness and motivation and are an integral part of memory creation.

Dennis the Caveman was a recipient of this good fortune; his (and our) neurotransmitters were tuned to seek good things and avoid the bad. Let's take a closer look at what some of these neurotransmitters residing in our body actually do.

*Dopamine*, for example, is a neurotransmitter that has a direct effect on our motivation and reward mechanism. It kicks in when we think we are going to be rewarded for taking some form of action. It is our "motivation chemical." When we anticipate something pleasurable, dopamine is released into our body; when we're pursuing something we desire, dopamine is what keeps us motivated to continue pursuing it. It drives the thrill of the chase.

Unfortunately, our brain releases dopamine into our neural pathways regardless of whether the pleasure we seek is considered good or bad.

For example, drug addiction is usually associated with a spike in dopamine. Dopamine plays many other roles in influencing our behavior and actions, such as our movements and attention span, but arguably none is as important for the survival of our species as its role as our motivation chemical.

## Why the Desire to Keep from Starving Is Important in Other Ways

The neurotransmitters in the body are triggered when we pursue a reward in anticipation of being satisfied. In our early ancestral days, the pursuit of food and what resulted (i.e., survival) was necessary. So humans ultimately developed motivation for the hunt. Without motivation, we would never have left our caves in search of food, and that would have been the end of us as a species. In addition to the motivation to seek food, getting the actual prize itself (the food) also provided positive feedback and resulted in a good feeling. Together, the desire to pursue the prize and the feeling resulting from the actual prize itself were driven by the neurotransmitters in our bodies.

If we were to take a look at what was going on in Dennis the Caveman's brain one morning, we might have observed the firing of neurotransmitters into his system that triggered a strong motivation to eat; he was hungry. This primal motivation was to prevent him from starving and withering away. But Dennis was motivated to hunt for any form of food to keep himself and his fellow cave people alive. Dopamine and other chemicals in his body flowed through his system and motivated Dennis the Caveman to go out into the danger zone and hunt. But that's not all. The motivation was driven by his understanding that the end result of this chase would be a juicy filet of mammoth; that is, food. And who wouldn't be motivated by that? (Perhaps vegetarian cavemen; but that is another matter.) So, Dennis, fueled by the neurotransmitters released in his body, continued the hunt in his strong desire to stay alive. He knew—and we'll get to the knowing part next—that his hunt would be rewarded with the desired experience. He would eat.

## Did You Know?

> Approximately 95 percent of our serotonin receptors are located in the gut, which is also considered our second brain. So, when you feel something is right or wrong in your gut, you may want to pay a little more attention to that feeling and "go with your gut."

**Important Points to Remember**

1. Once basic needs and comfort are met, having more money is not directly tied to increased long-term happiness.
2. Experiences are the building blocks of our lives. Experiences are what make our lives worth living - not our material possessions, and can lead to increased levels of happiness in our lives.
3. Chemicals, called neurotransmitters, are at the center of our thinking, behavior, and feelings – including motivation, sadness, and happiness.
4. The same neurotransmitters that kept our caveman and cavewoman ancestors alive are still important today and are the basis of *SFL Planning*.

# A WALK DOWN MEMORY LANE

*"A memory is a photograph taken by the heart to make a special moment last forever."*

--Unknown

## THE IMPORTANCE OF MEMORIES IN OUR LIVES

But it wasn't enough just to be motivated. Human development, making progress in life and survival, depended on learning from experiences and remembering them for future application. The brain evolved to differentiate between bad and good experiences and to respond accordingly. As it turns out, those powerful neurotransmitters in our bodies not only play a role in our motivation, but they are also involved in memory making as well as memory recall.

Perhaps you've read about the neurotransmitter *serotonin* and the role it plays in balancing our moods. But this chemical also plays a significant role in our memory and learning processes. When we go through an experience, learn a new topic, smell something we like or don't like, hear a catchy tune, or taste something delicious, the neurons in our body fire off serotonin, which helps create and anchor the new memory. If we go back to Dennis the Caveman and his hunt for food, his survival was based on remembering what he had learned as a young cave boy accompanying the men on their hunting excursions. He learned how to track the mammoth, how to stalk it, how to take it down, and how to run like crazy when things didn't work out as planned. He essentially learned what worked and what didn't, based on his experiences. It's the experiences we have that teach us what we need to know as we age so that we reach the point in time where we have conscious memories of those experiences.

The process of memory making starts when one or more of our senses are triggered by an event or experience. What's particularly interesting is the role emotions play in the memory-making process. How emotional an event is will determine the levels of neurotransmitters used and ultimately how well you remember the experience. The greater the number of senses, the more neurotransmitters are released, and the greater the memory imprint.

Most people are not familiar with the different types of memories. But understanding them will help you understand why *SFL Planning* is different from other planning systems and why it can lead to a happier and more memorable life. There is still much to discover about how the brain works, but it is generally understood that there are two types of memories: *implicit* and *explicit* (and explicit memories can further be subdivided into two varieties: *episodic* and *flashbulb*). In the sections that follow, we explore the fascinating world of memories and why making memories is so important to *SFL Planning*.

## THE DIFFERENT TYPES OF MEMORIES

### Implicit Memory

*Implicit memory* refers to what we know and what comes naturally to us. Implicit memories are deeply imprinted in our subconscious and include such basic activities as speaking, moving, and eating. We rely on implicit memories to perform our daily activities of living: tying our shoes, driving a car, riding a bicycle, reading, and even typing on our computer keyboards without looking at the keys. All these activities are accomplished without conscious thought; we don't purposely have to remember implicit memories. When needed, or called upon, they're there.

It's difficult to function in life without implicit memories. Going back to our Dennis the Caveman example, he didn't have to consciously remember how to walk or run. And he likely didn't have to do much recalling when he sharpened his spear. After sharpening his weapon numerous times, he had learned to do so without consciously thinking about it. After a while, those things just "come naturally."

Likewise, you are using your implicit memory to read this text.

**Explicit Memory**

*Explicit memory*, however, is information you have to consciously work to remember. When you are trying to intentionally remember something like a grocery list or where you parked your car or left your car keys, this information is stored in your explicit memory. We use these memories every day as well, from remembering information for a meeting to recalling the date and time of a doctor's appointment. When you say you have something on the tip of your tongue, you are consciously trying to remember that information. This is your explicit memory at work. One specific type of explicit memory crucial to *SFL Planning* and the most exciting one is *episodic memory.*

**Episodic Memory**

*Episodic memories* are your memories of specific events and include experiences such as your first date with someone special, the birth of your child, or your first day at work. Episodic memory is a person's unique recollection of a meaningful event—or an episode. People are usually able to associate particular details with an episodic memory, such as how they felt, time and place, and other facts. These types of memories trigger neurotransmitters and generate the most emotions.

Researchers believe that emotions play a critical role in which events we remember and how vividly we remember them. You are more likely to remember a roller-coaster ride, your wedding day, or a scary movie because of the sensations that are part of the event. Your brain treats them as distinct episodes and attaches emotion to them.

In its simplest form, episodic memory is analogous to a snapshot from one's past experience. Similarly, episodes that are more complicated are compared to movies stored within the mind. How often do you remember a time in your past and while remembering it, it feels like you are watching a movie?

**Flashbulb Memory**

*Flashbulb memory* is another type of explicit memory. It's described as an extremely emotionally charged memory due to the intensity of the experience. Flashbulb memories are so sudden and extraordinary that you remember many of the factors and sensations surrounding the moment the memories were created.

A prototypical flashbulb memory is the 9/11 terrorist attack. Relative to many people's other memories, the 9/11 events are vivid and provide a contextual frame around the activities that were taking place around them and the companions they were with at the time the events occurred.

A flashbulb memory is described as a reel-of-footage type of memory where you have a clear sense of time, place, and the sensations you felt when the event occurred.

These memories have a very unusual aspect about them in that they have personal consequences; they have significantly impacted the way you think about your world. They are unmistakable in their power to create powerful emotions.

Many flashbulb memories are negatively charged as they typically shock you, your world, and your belief system. In addition to the events of 9/11, some other national flashbulb memories of significance are the Kennedy assassination, the Reagan assassination attempt, and the Columbia shuttle explosion.

Unfortunately, you most likely also have personal and tragic flashbulb memories unique to you, which we all have experienced during our lives.

But there are also positive flashbulb memories, moments that were unexpected but left powerful imprints; for example, seeing, in real-time, extraordinary acts of kindness or heroism, or any of the following, which deserve some discussion.

## The Firsts in Your Life

The interesting thing about the firsts in your life is that there is an element of expectation and even preplanning and planning that have led up to the event and experience. But although you planned and prepared for this event, its actual impact is far beyond what you anticipated.

I'm talking about those events in your life, such as the first date you had with your first true love, your wedding, the birth of your first child, the marriage of that first child… so many things; too many to list here. These deal with human relationships. But there are other first experiences, solo in nature, that also touch you deeply.

You can envision, just from your own life, these types of powerful experiences. Perhaps it was the first time you got behind the wheel and drove on your own; or, for the more adventurous among us, perhaps it was the first time you went sky diving or climbed that mountain or went bungee jumping.

Seeing things for the first time can also create an impression, especially if there is a feeling of 'awe.' Here is an excerpt from something by author Dennis Lowery that, with his permission, I've adapted, which captures the essence of the moments and places that make you feel:

A scene. A place. A perfect moment that touched you deeply inside. And it filled you with wonder at how beautiful our world is, how vast its history, the unique people and places and how special it is to be there in that moment. In that location. *One of those places and moments from my experience:*

Gibraltar, as I watched the sun ease down and day turn to night. I followed the moonrise from my hotel room balconies that faced the Straits and the Atlantic and the other the Mediterranean. I thought of all the ships that had transited that relatively narrow opening as I had just done for the third time. I felt a sense, and appreciation, of the history of that unique geographic feature in our world.

## Scary or Frightening Moments Also Leave Impressions

One of the fascinating things about fear is that despite its primary function—to help us get out of dangerous, physically threatening situations—many of us are still drawn to these situations. Just think of all the favorite pastimes that are fueled by our attraction to fear:

bungee jumping, playing extreme sports, and riding roller-coasters to name a few.

This can be explained in part by the activity of chemical messengers, the neurotransmitters that we previously discussed, which carry signals between neurons in the brain and body. Some scientists believe thrill-seeking daredevils get more enjoyment out of such fear-inducing activities because their levels of dopamine increase more than normal during these experiences, resulting in intense feelings of pleasure or euphoria.

### DID YOU KNOW?

> Why do we remember frightening events so well? Fearful situations cause the release of stress neurotransmitters and hormones. These chemicals activate the flight, fight, or freeze response, which includes an increase in heart rate to facilitate the delivery of blood to working muscles. They also stimulate a brain structure called the amygdala.
>
> One function of the amygdala may be to assign significance to experiences, particularly those that are frightening and life-threatening, and then to enhance the ability of other brain regions to consolidate memories of those events. The selective nature of our memories makes sense; our very survival may depend upon learning the lessons from life-threatening episodes.

## The Sound and Music that Spark Us

*"We do not remember days; we remember moments."*
--Cesare Pavese

Have you ever smiled when you heard a song that you haven't heard in a while? Did you remember some of the good times associated with the song? Neurotransmitters are involved in this emotion-creating recollection process.

When you recollect memories, you are firing off neurotransmitters throughout your brain at levels almost equivalent to the original event. From happy to sad, from angry to motivated, these tiny chemicals are the juices that make you feel this way. It's no surprise that the levels of emotions directly influence your ability to remember sounds and songs that are associated with an experience.

Let's go back and visit our favorite caveman. You can imagine Dennis the Caveman tracking down a group of woolly mammoths when all of a sudden, he hears a loud sound from his right—the screeching and haunting roar of a saber-toothed tiger. And he can see out of the corner of his eye that it is moving fast.

If we were to take a look into Dennis's brain at this exact time, we would see a flood of neurotransmitters being released into his body.

Certain ones are preparing his body and creating the fight-flight-freeze response. Others are elevating his emotions and creating memories—and given the elevated sense of arousal, this is going to be a long-lasting memory.

The question for Dennis the Caveman—and for many like him during that time—is whether he will survive to learn from this experience.

Our bodies and underlying chemical system were honed to remember what was good and what was bad, which contributed a great deal to our survival. While we may not need to worry about saber-toothed tigers jumping us in the African savannah, we still retain that experience–memory creation mechanism.

So, let's just pretend that everything turned out well for Dennis the Caveman, and he eventually got his dinner. A peek into his brain would have shown he was rewarded with a drip of dopamine, which would have given him a feel-good emotion and positively reinforced his hunting experience and memory. Thanks to that, this human ancestor lived on for another day.

Regardless of how busy our lives become, we have the choice to make it memorable. Later in the book, you will learn how *SFL Planning* facilitates the making of happy and meaningful memories through experiences.

**Important Points to Remember**

1. Both implicit and explicit memories, which we make through experience, factor into how we act, what we know, and what is important to us.
2. Neurotransmitters are involved in the process that creates the feelings of motivation and drive in us as well as in the process that produces positive feelings when we achieve our goals.
3. The survival of the human species depended on learning from experiences–in particular dangerous ones, and remembering them in future situations. SFL Planning uses the same mechanism when creating positive memories that we cherish and remember over and over again.
4. Neurotransmitters play a critical role in both the emotion-creating process and in memory making. The more emotional the experience, the longer lasting the memory.

# WHY IS IT SO HARD TO STAY HAPPY?

*"A true saying it is, Desire hath no rest, is infinite in itself, endless, and as one calls it, a perpetual rack, or horse-mill."*

--St. Augustine

Most humans are running in place or running to keep up with someone or something just ahead of them. We're not happy (or can't stand still), and we always feel behind. Or perhaps we feel like we live inside M.S. Escher's artwork titled, "Relativity" where up is always ahead of us and always another set of stairs to climb. Eventually we start to sense that the stairs all lead to nowhere.

British psychologist Michael Eysenck referred to this as the hedonic treadmill theory. He compared the pursuit of happiness to a person on a treadmill who has to keep walking just to stay in the same place and continually work to maintain a certain level of happiness. But it's not a chase and it's not a race. There is no competition—just a human being on a gerbil wheel, or in this case, a treadmill. We are running awfully damn hard only to stay at the same level of (un)happiness.

The good news is *this is our choice – and we do have a choice.* Only we can make ourselves climb on that treadmill and go-go-go until we're exhausted emotionally, physically, and spiritually. Undoubtedly, many people gauge their self-value and accomplishments in life by the things they own. Their acquisitions serve as status symbols. However, we know from research – and our own personal experience, that material goods don't provide the lasting happiness we all seek.

What makes us happy is what's inside us—how we feel about who we are and what we've done, and a large part of that is shaped by our life experiences. And you can create them for no or almost no cost. When you realize that and try it in real time, in the real world, you understand how powerful experiences and memories are in becoming truly happy and content. Even experiential purchases (money spent on doing) tend to provide more enduring happiness than material purchases (money spent on having).

Again, keep in mind not all experiences require that you spend money to achieve happiness—in fact, some of your best ones will not cost anything at all. Most people, when they do finally decide to get off that treadmill—whether intuitively or through guidance—will see that they can create a much happier life by shifting their efforts to living the types of experiences that actually have a lasting effect. And this is not accomplished by chasing bright, shiny, expensive things that in and of themselves have little intrinsic value to our happiness and true quality of life.

The bottom line on the topic of hedonic adaptation is that even if you get a spike of happiness from buying a brand new gadget (or winning the lottery), we typically adapt and go back to our original level of happiness. So even as a person makes more money, expectations and desires rise in tandem, which results in no permanent net gain in happiness. I want to reinforce the point that purchasing new things is not necessarily bad, it's not bad at all, and can actually have a "retail therapy" effect on you. But if you want to create lasting happiness, you won't find it in a box (or bag).

There is a story from Japanese folklore called *The Stonecutter*. It makes for interesting reading on why it's so hard to remain content and how sometimes, when trying to change to become happy, but doing it in the wrong way—a flawed approach—can have the wrong consequences. It contends—and thus closely mirrors the negative aspect of hedonic adaptation—that there is no lifestyle or life that does not derive from consequences, and that life includes trials and experiences no matter who you are or what profession you choose.

As the story goes, the stonecutter mistakenly abandons the benefits of his life through the magic of a spirit that dwells on the mountain that is believed to make men rich when it appears before them.

The lure and the trappings of wealth were powerful in the mind of the stonecutter. He is happy at the beginning of the story, but questions what he's done with his life and who he is as a person. He starts to desire things he'd seen the wealthy have; they had so much when he had so little.

He asks the mountain spirit to change what type of person he is, to give him what the rich have. The spirit accommodates him, making change after change until he himself becomes a large rock. And then one day, he looks down at a happy stonecutter, just as he had once been. Just before he is broken by the man's pick, he realizes he chased too much, wanted all that the wealthy had, for all the wrong reasons.

A link to the full tale is included at the end of this book in the appendix should you wish to read it.

## Not Depressed? Great! But Are You Happy?

The study of depression far outweighs the study of happiness. And while there has been more research done on depression, there has been significant progress in the research on what contributes to happiness. There is far more interest today than ever on happiness and how our brain functions during times of happiness. And this is good, as the studies are starting to show how we can positively influence our state of well-being.

It's becoming better studied, understood, and documented that a small number of important factors—though individually unique—most heavily affect happiness. Happiness and excitement are personal. You may not be a fan of college football, but you may enjoy the lights and buzz of a top-notch Broadway show or an ethereal night at the ballet. The important point is that during those moments, something is happening in your brain that causes it to fire off those neurotransmitters that increase happiness and creates memories. And so while we are getting smarter on what creates positive feelings in us, we have been awfully slow to take advantage of this knowledge. Our inability, or unwillingness, to change and adopt these learnings has been a barrier to achieving greater heights of well-being.

Life is complicated today, far more so in the twenty-first century than in the world our ancestral cavemen lived in. We not only have to earn money to live (our modern-day equivalent of hunting for food), we also have distractions and an often destructive "busyness" of everyday life. Yes, "busyness." There are so many things that demand our time and attention in our over-connected, 24/7/365 life. And many of us have brought that busyness into our lives. Or certainly, perhaps unintentionally, we have let our lives become established in that pattern; and it exhausts us. Though we may not be depressed about our lives, that does not mean we are truly happy or can't be happier.

I can't speak for anyone but myself and those I know who've shared similar thoughts. Sometimes, we reach a point where we feel life is okay; it's acceptable. Sure, we have some nagging thoughts about "What if?" or "If I only had…," but our lives are not terrible. We're not unhappy; we're not depressed. *But we're also not really, really happy.* We've hit the mean (mathematically) in our life. The "mean" in math is the average; you're in the middle of the road, so to speak.

## Reaching an Inflection Point

An inflection point is a time of significant change in a situation—a turning point. It's the convergence of all that has happened to you in life—all the experiences and their memories—that become a catalyst for change.

I still vividly remember when I reached my own inflection point. For the majority of my working life, my story was a good one. By most measures, I was living a good life. I was achieving important, positive career and personal goals. I worked hard and made sacrifices to achieve relative success, and I earned a very good living. For many years, I assumed continuing to work at that level and hitting my next professional goal would create a peace of mind where I could finally relax and enjoy the fruits of my labor. There was no single thing I could point to in my personal life or career that I could say was not going in a positive direction. I was enjoying my professional career and I had a strong family life, especially with two little kids in the house. And yet—as I'm sure many of you have felt, too—that general sense of "I've arrived" and true happiness, seemed just out of reach—off in the distance.

I should have felt more content and at peace, but I didn't. I wondered if I ever would. It wasn't until 2011 when I came across an excellent book, *59 Seconds: Change Your Life in Under a Minute,* by Richard Wiseman that I learned that I have been thinking about happiness the wrong way, and in particular, my own role in increasing my happiness.

In the chapter titled "Happiness," one of the many engaging and thought-provoking chapters in the book, Wiseman describes the research findings showing how life experiences impact and promote happiness in a person's life. This simple point resonated with me like an early morning alarm clock: shockingly loud, beyond annoying, and urgent.

That one chapter jarred my thinking to such a degree that it was an inflection point in the way I approached life and ushered in a completely new way of thinking for me.

At that point in my life, I knew I was not purposely creating enough of the experiences I should have been. I was not only looking back and finding my life lacking experiences, I wasn't looking forward to exciting experiences, either.

I knew I could create more of those experiences for myself that are fundamental to better relationships, more joy, and greater peace of mind. There was an emotional element missing from what I wanted out of my life, the zest and variety that makes life so much more vivid and exciting.

It would be a few years later, when I also learned from other research studies how certain types of experiences have an even greater impact on your happiness than others, but at the time, I already knew I was onto something that could be invaluable for me.

As I mentioned, there is more research today on what happiness means to each of us than there has been in the past. The science and research on what makes us happy (the underpinnings of why *SFL Planning* works) are also becoming more newsworthy.

What you're reading now will help you enormously to recognize, and act on, what you can do to get beyond the "mean," the merely average. I don't think any of us wants to experience a merely average life.

## Creating Intentional Happiness

Scientists have known for decades that a large part of our temperament is genetically pre-determined. They determined this by cleverly studying the personalities of identical twins – specifically those sets that were separated at birth and therefore had different environments growing up, and found that about 50 percent of our happiness -- or unhappiness -- can be traced to our genes. This happiness set point comes from our genetic makeup—our predisposition of how happy we feel. (Yes, we in fact can blame our parents for this.) That and other related innate factors also determine when and how often brain chemicals are released in our bodies.

Building on those findings, University of California-Riverside psychology professor Dr. Sonja Lyubomirsky's research indicates that another 10 percent of our happiness is due to our current circumstances, either by choice or happenstance. Factors like our economic condition, our occupations, marital situations, income levels, and the like all affect our happiness, not only in the present but also our future outlook. What we believe the future holds for our current circumstances plays a role in our well-being. A good attitude will positively influence your happiness; conversely, a negative outlook lowers it. How you respond to these circumstances, how much control you feel you have over them, will influence your state of mind. And if you've hit a rough patch in life, whether you feel there is a light at the end of the tunnel or if you can make lemonade out of lemons, also affects your overall happiness. It is truly your mindset that shapes your well-being. And this can be learned, too. How you view your situation and how you respond are up to you. And it does make a difference in your happiness.

That leaves us with the remaining 40 percent. This is a significant number to leave to chance or to ignore. The research shows we can directly affect 40 percent of our personal level of satisfaction through intentional activity, which means what we purposely do and the actions we take in our lives. Clearly this is worth going after – even negligent if we don't, if we want to reach higher levels of happiness. And that 40 percent is precisely what the *SFL* approach to planning targets.

To do this, *SFL Planning* integrates three fundamental concepts focused on impacting the 40 percent. These have become the *SFL Pillars* which you will read about later in this book. You'll also find examples of *SFL Planning* in action where the three *SFL Pillars* are brought to life. They show how intentional activities designed to maximize the planning and enjoyment of our experiences lead to memorable moments that are the chapters of our life story. I know that some of you reading this will recognize some of those examples and realize that perhaps unintentionally you were following (and enjoying) the *SFL Planning* principles. Imagine what life will be like and the joy you will experience when you actively and intentionally create a game plan and begin to follow it purposefully.

<u>DID YOU KNOW?</u>

> A comprehensive study from the University of Illinois in 2011 found that happy people tend to live longer and experience better health than their gloomy peers. So, if you want to live to see that medical breakthrough that will give you a few more years of life, you better start smiling more today.

**Important Points to Remember**

1. Not being depressed is not the same as being happy. Many of us in life are at a stage or point where "life is what it is…" and we're okay with that. It's not great, and we are not truly happy, but we're just okay. *SFL Planning* teaches us that we can change this; we don't have to settle for a ho-hum life story. We can make it remarkable.
2. We all have a genetically disposed happiness set point and so while we have emotional highs and

lows throughout life, we typically adapt and revert back to the level of happiness we were at before.
3. While 50 percent of our happiness -- or unhappiness -- can be traced to our genes, we can positively affect 10 percent through our outlook on life and the remaining 40 percent through intentional actions.
4. The pursuit of happiness through material purchases will put you on the hedonic treadmill – a fruitless and never-ending journey. However, certain types of experiences can increase your overall well-being. Intentionally pursuing these experiences can positively affect your happiness.

# LIVING LIFE WITH ZEST

*"If you have zest and enthusiasm you attract zest and enthusiasm. Life does give back in kind."*

--Norman Vincent Peale

So, now you know whether it is extreme joy or fear, that awesome roller-coaster ride, or watching a scary movie, at the moment you had these experiences, your brain was flooded with neurotransmitters.

Knowing this is important because *SFL Planning* focuses on intentionally creating emotionally exciting experiences that tap into parts of our primitive brain in a positive, constructive way.

We do this by accessing evolutionary brain structures called the limbic system, considered the emotional epicenter of the human brain. This part of our brain helps form our memories and integrates emotion so we know whether it was a healthy and happy memory or a bad unhappy one.

Two parts of the limbic system, the amygdala and the hippocampus, are particularly important to *SFL Planning*. Emotions are primarily produced in the amygdala, which, by the way, also helps store memories that are emotionally charged.

The more emotionally exciting your experience, the more the amygdala is at work and the longer lasting the memory.

Our memories are created, formed, and classified in the hippocampus, whose primary function is to create memories and store them long-term. We also use the hippocampus when we remember and share with others our memories and experiences.

It's clear why we would want to plan in such a way that specifically taps into these parts of our brain and create positive memories. By doing this, we impact the 40 percent of our happiness that we control through intentional activities.

The *SFL Planning* process will guide you to think about the positive experiences you want to make memorable so you can actually plan them. I'll go through this in more detail later in the book.

As you will read in this book, there are certain types of experiences—and not all experiences are created equal—that lead to a greater level of happiness and satisfaction in life.

The primary premise supporting the *SFL Planning* approach is that you will actively and purposefully plan those specific experiences that fire the neurotransmitters associated with feeling good and making memories.

So, while we may be busy people, we can still add these types of experiences to our lives, but only if we make that our intention.

## Adding Emotion to Help Achieve Goals

A surprising factor to effectively reaching goals is to consider emotions and put them to work for you. Many people set goals that are as inspirational as a doorknob. It's no wonder people often don't reach them. But you can improve your chances by making emotion your ally in reaching your goals. Adding certain emotional elements into your goal setting can add a surprising, supporting boost to your efforts. This can help with even the most stubborn of common goals.

For example, if you are not someone naturally blessed to *always* be trim and fit, odds are you've dealt with the following goal. Let's say you want to lose ten pounds. What meaning do you put into losing ten pounds? Is it the actual number of pounds you want to lose that gets you excited? Or is it the way you expect to feel when you are ten pounds lighter, the increased confidence you have when you walk into a room? Will it be how you envision your clothes will feel and look on you, and what clothes you will actually get to wear? Is it the relief knowing your doctor will give you a clean bill of health or the feeling that you are doing what you can to be healthy for your spouse and children? Or conversely, do you dread how you will feel when you put on those suddenly tight pants? Do you hear your doctor's stern admonishment? Negative emotions can also motivate you to action.

What if you thought about losing weight in a different way than just thinking about the pounds? How about focusing on attaining certain feelings? Losing a targeted number of pounds is good for many health reasons, but for me, it's really about how I expect to feel in my clothes and the sense of being fit. I don't think about the number of pounds I'm going to lose; instead, I imagine how I will feel when my pants are looser (or how they won't be so stifling and uncomfortable). And no, I don't cheat by buying larger pants, or rationalize (usually) that the pants somehow shrunk in the laundry! I don't focus on the calories or my weight, those are meaningless to me. But I do focus on how I will feel sitting comfortably, without my pants pinching or threatening to pop a button. That's much more impactful and motivating to me.

While losing weight is not the point of *SFL Planning*, with the right approach to planning, losing those ten pounds can also be fun. What if you were to plan exercise routines, such as hiking or swimming, and make them part of family outings? It doesn't have to be anything elaborate, but try adding something fun and different to your regular workout schedule. Would that slight change of perspective make a difference in how you would view going about losing those ten pounds?

What if you also approached the eating part of the equation with a different lens? Instead of facing off with raw vegetables and other not-so-tasty options, how about planning cooking nights with your family or friends and making healthier but more exotic types of dishes? Those dinners – and the actual making of the dinners, could become more like events you actually look forward to. These are just some examples to demonstrate where the addition of emotion can be integrated into your life in even unpleasant undertakings (e.g. dieting) to create positive memories. Adding this type of positive emotional element may not be for everyone, but it is effective for many.

As you can see, experiences, memories, and emotions are integral parts to *SFL Planning*. If you were to stop right now and start applying some of what you have already read, you would be well on your way to enjoying many of the benefits from *SFL Planning*. Yet, in the next section, I'll go through the key SFL concepts in more detail and provide you more information that will take what you have learned to another level.

**Important Points to Remember**

1. Experiences that come with or are associated with strong emotions tap into parts of our primitive brain and create vivid imprints of memories.
2. We impact our personal happiness through emotionally positive experiences.

3. Emotional content is an integral part to *SFL Planning* and one you will actively engage in creating in your life.
4. Adding certain emotional elements into your goal setting can also add a surprising, supporting boost to your efforts.

# SET FOR LIFE PILLARS

# PILLAR 1 – EXPERIENCES

*"The joy of life comes from our encounters with new experiences, and hence there is no greater joy than to have an endlessly changing horizon, for each day to have a new and different sun."*

--Christopher McCandless

### ALL EXPERIENCES ARE NOT CREATED EQUAL

The concept of life experiences is a linchpin to the overall *SFL Planning* approach. There are numerous studies and articles available that cover the value of experiences over material goods when it comes to increasing a person's happiness. But are there differences in the types of experiences? Essentially, everything we do is an experience, but it's obvious that not all experiences are equally as important or as meaningful. And we certainly don't remember every experience we have. The question is whether we can identify the qualities of the types of experiences that, based on research studies, lead to a higher level of happiness and overall contentment with life. I believe we can.

If you are looking to add more meaning and fun

into your life, you have to plan the type of experiences that create a bigger impact. "Directed pleasure" (as identified and proven by self-reflection) can help achieve our highest level of happiness. This is far more important than a life guided by items on a checklist. When you purposely create experiences, you add more enthusiasm and zest to your life, and it can make a huge difference in a life worth remembering

## A *SFL* Experience Will Make You Happy

The reality is all of us come from the same basic biological origin, regardless of where we live in the world. Our DNA reaches back to that common ancestor, so it's probably not that surprising that there are qualities we all share that contribute to our happiness. Researchers have studied people around the globe and have identified a set of qualities that describes the types of experiences that can create long-lasting positive emotions in our lives. These are the guiding qualities of the *SFL Experience*s. This is not to say there aren't other types of experiences or other things people can do to add joy to their lives. It would be ludicrous to think otherwise. But this specific set of qualities—described below—provides the tangible foundation for the type of experiences you can actually plan into your life so you actively increase your happiness.

## Qualities of a *SFL* Experience

Listed below are the key characteristics of experiences, which research has shown lead to increased levels of happiness in a person's life. They are specific, under our control, and tie to how we are wired as humans. And while joyful moments often come during impromptu and unplanned times, the opportunity for all of us is to intentionally plan and incorporate more of these types of experiences into our lives so that we take an active role in increasing our long-term well-being. Simply stated, we don't have to leave everything to chance. We can proactively do something knowing it will positively impact our lives.

Listed below are the key qualities of an *SFL Experience* – one that can increase your happiness and the frequency of positive emotions.

Key Qualities:

1. An *SFL Experience* includes physical activity. You are in motion during an *SFL Experience.*
2. An *SFL Experience* adds variety to your life. In other words, it is in some way different and not commonplace in your life. An *SFL Experience* stands out and is often the first time you do something.
3. An *SFL Experience* is shared with others. One of the

learnings from research was the fun and camaraderie that comes from doing something together as well as the telling (and retelling) the story of the experience.
4. An *SFL Experience* is personally meaningful, fun and aligns with your interests. If you are not interested in camping, a camping-related experience is simply not going to add much excitement or joy to your life. This is not to say you shouldn't try something new to see if you enjoy it and get excited by it, but if you know you do not enjoy something, the odds are that the activity isn't going to be enjoyable.

The combination of these characteristics will have a big impact on increasing your long-term well-being. This is important, and it can change how you view planning and the purpose planning has in your life. Shifting from a checklist model to one where you plan meaningful experiences will bring joy and contentment to your life. In other words, add the things to your life that make you happy and a happier person. In effect, you will go from managing tasks to writing your life story filled with experiences that you will cherish and share with others.

Let's take a more detailed look at each of the qualities that make up an *SFL Experience*.

## Make It an Active Experience

*"Action may not always bring happiness; but there is no happiness without action."*

--Benjamin Disraeli

An active experience is literally about physical movement; motion gets our bodies responding and the neurotransmitters firing in our brains. Of course, there are many things you can enjoy sitting still. Most if not all of us enjoy watching TV from our favorite chair or while stretching out on the couch. But those are transitory, transient, and passive experiences that do not typically drop anchor in our memories. However, you can create an active experience if you are actively out and about and doing something out of the ordinary, such as going to the theater.

Again, it's about being in motion and exposed to the stimuli of movement, action, and the changing environment around you. Physical motion engages your brain on many levels and lends heightened sensitivity to your experience.

As you read about another quality in the next section, the *active experience* is typically part of a unique or *novel experience*. And that is fertile ground for the seed of memories to be planted.

## Make It Stand Out

*"Do not be too timid and squeamish about your actions. All life is an experience."*

--Ralph Waldo Emerson

Another quality of an *SFL Experience* is that it is not common, mundane, or routine. As a matter of fact, the types of experiences that lead to increased happiness levels are oftentimes those that make people uncomfortable.

It is a personally unusual or uncharacteristic experience; for example, a typically shy or introverted person sings karaoke at a club.

By doing something uncharacteristic or unique, we often ratchet up our level of happiness and memory making by going outside our comfort zones. So in short, a little nervousness may go a long way to making you a lot happier.

It's good to push beyond and expand our familiar boundaries. This makes a lot of sense. When you consider having a memorable life—one that creates stories to talk about, relive, and retell with friends—the unique, once-in-a-lifetime experiences are what stand out. You use more of your emotional capacity during those not-business-as-usual experiences.

Doing something outside of what's normal for you leads to increased emotional engagement. And that is proven to lead, ultimately, to increased well-being—even if you are nervous while you are in the middle of the experience.

It's that excitement that writes the chapters in your life story. And, when you share these experiences with someone else—bingo! You get an extra positive charge and a sense of exhilaration.

Here's an exercise: Close your eyes and think back to your high school (or college) days. What do you remember? I'm betting most, if not all, the days you remember are in some ways different than the run-of-the-mill, normal days.

On the days, you do remember more often than not, something unique and different occurred on those days. Something makes those days stand out. The clearest memories are those that have more emotions attached to them.

When I think back over the many years of my career, there are actually very few "normal" days I remember or have a reason to recall. While some would say, I have a bad memory, and that may be true, it's more likely the emotions tied to the regular, run-of-the-mill days weren't high.

But on days having high-stakes presentations, for example, I absolutely remember them, crystal clear. That's how we are wired. The more emotions, the longer lasting the memory.

## Make It a Shared Experience

*"You can design and create, and build the most wonderful place in the world. But it takes people to make the dream a reality."*

--Walt Disney

There is no way around this one. *Whether you are a people person or an extreme introvert, you need relationships to create and heighten your sense of happiness.* Blame it on evolution, but people are social animals. We needed it to survive as a species. It was very difficult, likely impossible, to survive those tough caveman days if you went out and faced the world solo. The odds were distinctly better if you went out in numbers.

Additionally, there is something uniquely inherent in humans about how good it feels to serve others. Lending a helping hand creates an emotional bond. Again, connecting it back to evolution, this feeling and inclination to help others likely comes from our cave-dweller days.

When everything was done as a group, those who survived the rugged environment were more inclined to help and be helped by others. I suspect those who got along with others in the tribe had better odds of survival.

So, we're wired to help others and it feels good

to do so. If you've ever participated in an charity event, such as a 5k run or a softball tournament, you know that the combination of having fun with other people and doing it for a good cause gives you a euphoric, feel-good feeling. You enjoy the experience and you're happy to talk about it later, which makes the feeling last even longer. Stories may come out of the experience which are shared days, weeks, or even years later.

### DID YOU KNOW?

> There are likely more similarities than differences between cultures regarding the importance of involving others in your experiences. Previous studies have shown that in the United States, introverts experience greater levels of happiness when they engage in extroverted behaviors like smiling at a passerby or calling an old friend.
>
> Study findings were published in the Journal of Research in Personality that state: "We are not the first to show that being more extroverted in daily behavior can lead to more positive moods. However, we are probably the first to extend this finding to a variety of cultures," said Timothy Church, PhD, professor of counseling psychology at Washington State University. So, don't worry about being outgoing and friendly in another country, it's universally welcomed!

Put aside the competitive aspect of it for now—and sure, winning makes it a little sweeter—but being with other people at an event for a good cause simply brings a sense of joy. Those magical moments and fun experiences activate inborn values that we as humans have so greatly benefited from in our past.

We are social beings who simply get something positive from being with other folks, and regardless of the circumstance—win or lose—we are energized by the fact that we are serving others and doing something good. It's a powerful combination. This epitomizes the *SFL Planning* principle of leveraging the power of experiences in your life to create a more fulfilling one rich with relationships.

## Make It Personally Meaningful and Fun

*"We don't stop playing because we grow old; we grow old because we stop playing."*

--George Bernard Shaw

People have different definitions of what *play* and *fun* means. What any one person considers fun and enjoyable likely comes from a mixture of personality, upbringing, skills, and past experiences and the emotions attached to them (of course). The important point is that an *SFL Experience* must be personally fun for you, i.e. you have fun doing it. The one caveat is you may need to do something for the first time to determine if you have fun doing it (see the second *SFL*

*Experience* quality). And in general, it's good to try a lot of different things to find out what you find fun and exciting, and what is not. So, while the specific experiences differ, the underlying common denominator is the same, we all like to have fun.

I know many associates and acquaintances who have careers where extensive travel is required and are frequently away from their families. In my own personal life, I typically traveled around forty-eight weeks a year and was away from my wife four days a week. So, it was an obvious choice that one of my priorities was planning fun experiences with my wife.

For example, I tried to exercise on a regular basis. A three-mile jog was my main workout. It wasn't until I started to purposely plan fun experiences involving exercising with my wife that I started to look at exercising as more than just an effort to stay fit. Rather than just jog for the sake of exercising, my wife and I started planning to run 5k races—ideally for charity. For the record, I run at the speed of a turtle, so finishing was typically the bar I set for myself. Looking for a race, the preparation, training, and actually running the 5k became a fun experience for both of us.

Once I realized how much I enjoyed the race events, I never looked at exercising the same way. Instead of finding it a chore to exercise just to check exercising off the list of things I had to do to keep fit, I was now looking at races as fun experiences my wife and I could do together.

Anchoring my exercise activities to fun, exciting, and shared experiences with my wife completely changed my outlook on exercise. It also added a new dimension to the things my wife and I talked about.

Sure, there was still talk about mortgages, repairs, and the kids' activities, but now we were also including conversations on upcoming races and the stories from the events themselves.

Here's another short exercise for you: Think through activities you really enjoy and see if you can combine them with a good cause. Personally, I enjoy a 5k run for charity; it is an awesome event for me.

It's even better if your friends are part of it. Running (or even fast walking) the race will likely take less than one hour, and yet the stories and memories will last so much longer than the run itself. These types of memories become embedded in our long-term memory.

An important point to note here is that it doesn't matter what you're doing on a day-in, day-out basis. As long as you are planning *SFL Experiences* regularly, you can enjoy greater levels of happiness in your life. They do not have to cost you anything; there's a countless number free of charge.

The more varied the experiences are, the more happiness you will find. To the extent your experiences include others, the more bonding moments you create, and the more memories to share.

As you think about experiences to plan, consider these factors. Look for those that are fun for you and serve others in some way. And do it with a family member or friend; sharing the experience will boost your level of happiness. Think of these experiences as future scrapbook material, and start planning the right type of experiences today.

## Did You Know?

> According to epigenetics, the study of inheritable changes in gene expression not directly coded in our DNA—our life experiences may be passed on to our children and our children's children.
>
> It was commonly thought that a new embryo's epigenome was erased and rebuilt from scratch, but studies show otherwise. Some of a parent's experiences can be passed down to their offspring through a process called epigenetic inheritance. In other words, certain genetic memories are passed on.
>
> So, if you are young and plan on having children, this is an added incentive to having happy and meaningful experiences. If you have children, make sure they too have wonderful experiences – they can have a positive impact on your grandchildren!

## Important Points to Remember

1. The concept of life experiences is a linchpin to the overall *SFL Planning* approach. If you are looking to add more meaning and fun into your life, you have to plan the type of experiences that create a bigger impact.
2. Not all experiences are the same, and it's important to be selective about the ones we want. Identify the specific types of experiences that are most important to you in order to raise the level of our happiness in your life.
3. There are certain characteristics for *SFL Experiences*, which lead to increased happiness and include the following: A. Physically active in nature, B. Are different and unique from your normal and everyday activities, C. Are shared with other people and D. Personally fun and meaningful to you.
4. Intentionally plan *SFL Experiences* into your life and enjoy greater feelings of happiness and fulfillment with others.

## It's All About the Story…

*"Do you wait for things to happen, or do you make them happen yourself? I believe in writing your own story."*

--Charlotte Eriksson

Stop thinking about your day, your week, your life as a checklist and start thinking about your life as a collection of experiences. One of the drivers behind the *SFL* approach to planning is that the experiences you plan will create your memories and ultimately your life story. We are at our core a collection of our experiences. The more memorable and pleasurable those experiences are, the more joy your life story will hold. There is no reason your life cannot be filled with stories you will remember, cherish, and want to share. Choose to plan your life in a way that promotes enriching experiences. Experiences turned into long-term, pleasurable memories are the bricks and mortar that create the foundation of our existence.

Ask yourself these questions about your life:

1. What experiences from my past do I cherish most?
2. What experiences do I want to have?
3. What memories do I want to create that will make me most happy in the future?

How you write your life story is up to you—it is yours to write. Consider this: How often do you find yourself sharing stories with friends, enjoying every part of it, even though you've told or heard it dozens of times? There is a unique quality to those memories to make you feel that way. Will your future experiences be as enjoyable, memorable, and fun? Or will they be dull and ordinary? What stories do you want to create that you will be able to share with others? You get one shot at life; there is no denying, every second, minute, hour, and day are going to pass forever. Once they're gone, they're gone, finished, over.

Being productive and efficient are powerful when it comes to the business of life, and being productive is certainly valuable when maximizing the time for you to do other things. But what you do with that available time will play a factor in your happiness. It's the experiences you have that will ultimately result in a more meaningful, happier, and memorable life.

Use your new understanding of the power of emotions as a guide to creating compelling experiences and memories that shape your future. Ask yourself, before your life is over, what are the experiences you want to have that will immeasurably deepen your life?

Some of you may struggle to remember a thing or two that was memorable from just last week; some won't be able to recall anything that stands out at all. Why is it so hard? The problem you might have with identifying a significant memory is because oftentimes, we don't *purposefully* look to create a memorable impact in our life stories.

Note, I said we don't look to "purposefully" make an impact. Let me explain why I used that word instead of "purposely": *purposely* means "on purpose."

It is a synonym of *intentionally*. When you *mean* to do something, you do it *purposely*. *Purposefully* means (1) with a sense of purpose, or (2) with determination. For example, when you are determined to ask your boss for a raise, you might walk into her office *purposefully*. I believe the context of *SFL Planning* purposefully expresses a stronger intent; it means there is a plan driving your purpose.

It can sound overwhelming and even preposterous to think you can actually plan your life story, but that is exactly what I'm saying you can do. It's what you can do to make your life more remarkable. Of course, you won't be planning your whole life at once, far from that, but you are going to be thinking differently about what you put in your planner.

If you adopt the *SFL Planning* strategies, you will thoughtfully and *purposefully* plan the experiences that will have an impact, the ones you can get excited about and provide meaning to your life. Later in the book, I will describe a question-driven process that will guide you as you do your planning using the *SFL* approach.

## Creating Memories from the Ordinary

Experiences are the crux of the *SFL* approach to planning. But what does that really mean? To bring oomph and meaning to your life, those experiences must matter and resonate with you. *This is personal.* It has to mean something to you, or said another way, you must find meaning in it. An experience such as going to Wrigley Field and enjoying a baseball game with the family can be an exciting and fun event. You can also have a more ordinary experience, such as going to a movie with your daughter on a Saturday afternoon. The point is, you don't have to wait for a once-in-a-lifetime event to have an *SFL Experience*.

Some of my fondest memories come from activities that could have been mundane and unremarkable had I not incorporated some of the qualities of an *SFL Experience* to convert them into meaningful experiences. For example, Saturday night TV became a special event with the kids; that two-hour slot became something I looked forward to and planned an evening around.

Clearly, it wasn't always about the movie itself. I was hooked by the event and family time. From picking the movie to popping the popcorn, a casual and fun dinner, and fluffing the couch pillows, the family all looked forward to movie night. What could have been simply a night of watching TV turned into a *Movie Night Spectacular Event,* an opportunity to share cherished time with my wife and kids. We looked forward as a family to doing these things together. It was special for me, but more importantly, it was special for my kids. The bottom line is this: when I'm long gone, I want my kids to remember those movie nights (and, selfishly, me too). And I hope they have the same kind of bonding experiences with their kids one day.

A movie night event might sound like making the commonplace bigger than it really is, and frankly, that is exactly the intent. Take the ordinary and make it a memorable experience. In this case, it was a movie night, but it can be a date night with the spouse or a Saturday beach day or family hike; the possibilities are endless. The more excitement you create leading up to the event, the better.

I asked my friend, Dennis Lowery, who is a true believer in *SFL Experience*s to write some examples from his life, both from the vantage point of a more common experience as well as an example where longer-term planning and anticipation were incorporated. Here is what he wrote:

### *Bogie Night with My Daughters*

My four daughters (ages twenty-six, eighteen, and twins that are fourteen) know Humphrey Bogart is my favorite actor from what I consider the Golden Age of Hollywood. I'm a writer and even wrote a blog piece about Bogie, and how though I like John Wayne, too… but…well, Bogie was just the best.

A few years ago, for my birthday on

December 18th, my daughters agreed to watch one of my favorite Bogart movies, *We're No Angels,* which I consider a Christmas movie.

At first, it was, "Okay, Dad... we'll sit and watch it with you—it's your birthday, after all."

Then, as they watched the movie, they laughed at all the right moments with the clever dialogue and sight gags and so on and appreciated its message of compassion and kindness (to those deserving it). At the end, all said, they really enjoyed it. Success! And a great evening together with my girls.

The next day in my office at home, I was writing and working...and stopped to check on what my youngest three daughters were up to.

They were in the family room, watching a movie on the big TV. It was *We're No Angels*. And they were laughing. Success! My birthday gift keeps on giving...

ED ELGARRESTA

# The Unplanned Story—Making the Most of a Bad Situation

Not all experiences are planned, and in many cases positive experiences—the proverbial silver lining—may come out of negative situations.

In 1992, Hurricane Andrew hit South Florida; it was a devastating storm that left many without homes. If you were lucky to be able to stay in your home, it was likely you did not have power. Hurricane Andrew came through August 24th, and it was hot. There wasn't much you could do. Roads closed; schools and companies closed—everything was shut down. Many families and friends grouped together, usually at the home that got electrical power first. Many neighbors worked together to clear out the debris from their roads.

During this time, you didn't have any conflicting schedules. No meetings to go to or anything else you could do but spend time with your family, neighbors, and friends, helping each other. While there was much to do to get things back to normal, during this time neighbors and friends bonded in an extraordinary way. Many shared memories, including positive ones, came out of the aftermath of Hurricane Andrew. While Hurricane Andrew was certainly a unique event—and there is every hope and prayer it never happens again—because of its enormity, the memories of those who lived through it will last forever. I'm sure this experience is shared by many who have gone through similar devastating situations across the globe. The same mechanism in our brain that is used in creating positive memories is also used during negative experiences. While we don't like to have these types of memories, they typically do leave deep and vivid imprints in our brains.

Whether you plan them or not, your life stories are either being written by you or for you—make no mistake about it. Whether you like it or not, *you* are the director of your life. The difference between being an active director in your life and a passive one is whether you are intentionally creating what you want versus "life just happening to you." Either way, your story becomes how you and others will remember your life. And like all stories, it will have a beginning, middle, and an end; what goes into the chapters between the first and the last page is up to you.

**Important Points to Remember**

1. While acquiring material possessions is not the basis for a happy and contented life, the quality of your experiences is.
2. We must create and plan specific types of experiences to establish the memories that can mean the most to us individually.
3. You are the ultimate director of your life story. You have the ability to create the memories of your life.

Your story becomes how you and others will remember your life.
4. Look for opportunities to create an enduring and positive story around even mundane and negative events.

# PILLAR 2 - ANTICIPATION

*"As a child, I was bonkers for Christmas. The entire month of December, I couldn't sleep at night from anticipation."*

--Rosecrans Baldwin

You now know about the importance of experiences in your life and how they align with your brain and body's mechanism. We've also discussed how and why positive memories can be made when high levels of excitement and emotions are part of those experiences. Another innate response the *SFL* approach to planning relies on to further increase your happiness is the concept of *anticipation* - the idea of looking forward to something.

Usually, we think of anticipation in a negative light. We worry about (anticipate) getting lost or think, "I'm going to forget where I parked my car." We anticipate rain or snow, traffic delays, waiting for a table at a busy, favorite, restaurant, and so on. You get the picture. In many respects, this is good if you consider and plan for those events. Certainly, just about all of us at one time or another have left our homes earlier than usual to beat the traffic. And we carry umbrellas just in case it rains.

We instinctively think this way. We're a species who survived by anticipating, watching for, worrying about, and avoiding, if possible, predators who wanted us for their main course. Our brains and chemical reaction systems are honed for survival and center on our internal fight-flight-freeze response to survive. This mechanism has served us very well to say the least. Some might say too well, as our fears and reactions to potential fear may outweigh reality.

### DID YOU KNOW?

The topic of anticipation is growing in popularity and importance as an emerging field of study at a global scale. The First International Conference on Anticipation was held in November, 2015 in Trento, Italy with the goal of exploring the interaction among anticipation, uncertainty and complexity. So, while anticipation is being used for global matters, it can also be applied to our own personal life to create positive emotions.

For example, the fear and anxiety associated with public speaking is clearly greater than it should be. However, part of the reason for this is our primeval brain. Standing in front of a large group to speak can be a harrowing experience, but it's certainly not a life-and-death one. Unfortunately, the primitive parts of our brain don't always realize the distinction. They shoot certain neurotransmitters and other chemicals into our systems, increasing our heart rate, making us breathe faster and sweat more. All are part of our basic survival response. When all we want is to run away, but public speaking requires us to stay put, we are forced to act against nature. We may feel threatened by the fear of rejection by the audience. After all, we are still social animals, and remember, cavemen and cavewomen kicked out of the clan probably didn't survive very long. But that particular fear no longer serves us in most circumstances in today's world. The fear of public speaking is a good example of how little control we sometimes have of our primeval brain.

## Anticipate Like a Child

What we typically don't do well as a species is anticipate good events. Certainly, we don't do it as often as we did when we were children. When was the last time you looked forward to a birthday party, a wedding, or a sporting event? And I mean, really looked forward to it. We did this when we were young, but as we get older, our anticipation time horizon becomes short. We are busier, more distracted, and our ability to look forward to something can be a bit rusty. As adults, we mostly focus on our daily and weekly checklists. But we can change that and grow younger in this aspect of our thinking and planning.

While planning experiences into our lives will in itself increase our happiness levels, we can take this to another level. Studies done at the University of

Colorado and Cornell University demonstrated people often derive more pleasure and excitement from the anticipation leading up to an experience than that of actually getting a material item. What can we learn from this?

We can purposely create and plan anticipatory events leading up to an experience to expand and amplify the happiness and memories associated with the overall experience. Some people are naturally inclined to plan this way; they identify activities and other events that build up the anticipation of the overall experience. However, many people look at the activities leading up to the experience as tasks that are in the way of the experience they desire. *SFL Planning* changes this.

*SFL Planning* is about coupling our instinctive sense of anticipation with our planned experiences. Why should we solely experience an event as something singular and only once it happens? We can plan in a way that incorporates memorable, anticipation-building activities that lead up to and *enhance the actual target SFL Experience*. This is something we may do in an ad hoc manner for some things, but we don't often consciously think about it systematically as part of how we plan.

What if you incorporated events into your planning that you can look forward to? What if you made those events into positive mini *SFL Experiences* as well? What if you can plan in such a way that creates events that, in turn, lead to a series of positive emotions? With what you are learning, you are going to do just that. You are going to plan memorable activities that lead to the target experience you desire, all of which will increase your overall happiness and contentment.

As you incorporate *SFL Planning* into your life, your mindset will be to look for opportunities to build positive anticipation; identify those activities and events that you can look forward to and get excited about. Later in the book, I will introduce the process and the types of questions you can ask yourself during your planning that will help you identify those types of anticipatory events.

## Build in Anticipation to Enrich Your Memories

The more deliberate you plan your experiences and all the elements leading up to the intended target *SFL Experience*, the more memorable the entire experience will become. Until it becomes second nature, try thoughtfully planning two or three anticipation-building intermediate events leading to your *SFL Experience*. This will help you train your brain to think this way until it becomes a natural way of planning. As you go through this process, you may think of it as preparing for your experience. But there is an important difference to how you think about the preparation.

In the classic sense, preparing often means creating and accomplishing a required checklist of items to achieve a goal. But in *SFL Planning*, your in-between steps aren't a checklist like that; instead, they are more akin to pre-events—thoughtful, emotional, mini-events that you plan in order to create an overall broader and deeper experience with added memories.

Something like a Saturday fishing trip with your son could include learning about the types of fish you are likely to catch, learning about and buying the type of bait or lure that attracts that type of fish, preparing the lines and hooks, checking into and preparing for the weather you're likely to encounter, and so on.

You get the picture. You not only build excitement and anticipation for the actual fishing trip and actually enjoy the preparation steps, but you also elevate them as part of the overall fishing trip experience you are creating with your son. You and your son will now have multiple memorable events of the fishing trip.

Another example for a mother and daughter event could be a night at the ballet. Let's agree that people who know something about the ballet they are going to see will probably enjoy it more. So, to build anticipation and make the night even richer, imagine a mother and her daughter together reading up on the history of the ballet, the story behind it, and the music. Learning about the dancers who will perform and even about the venue can also be another source of anticipation. Of course, there's also the pleasure of looking forward to dinner at a nice restaurant before the ballet. As you can see, it's more than just the event. There's also all the surrounding events leading up to the actual performance that the mother and daughter can cherish together.

Just as the father and son on their fishing trip, this mother and daughter are sharing bonding moments. And consider this (because these examples are not limited to gender-specific activities): How about the father taking his daughter to the ballet, and the mother taking her son on the fishing trip? How powerful would those experiences be? Both the mother and father would probably be out of their comfort zones—and their son and daughter would have a ringside seat to see them experiencing something new.

You, and those you shared these experiences with, will look back at these events and have far richer and deeper memories. This is how you create another piece of what becomes a memorable life. For some, this is a natural process; for others, this creates entirely new outlooks on their lives.

Here is a real-world example, also from Dennis Lowery, of not only how planning the big event—the target experience—adds happiness to our lives, but also how the things leading up to it do as well:

### *My Family's Great American Summer Vacation Road Trip Adventure*

My wife and I had talked about a family road trip for a couple of years. But we wanted to wait for our youngest children to be old enough to recall the trip and have memories that would undoubtedly develop from the experience.

The summer of 2006, our children were at a sweet spot in age, and we had a relatively narrow window for our family to do something like this. My oldest was seventeen, nearly eighteen, the next was ten, and our twins were five, almost six years old. The pressure point was our oldest; another year and she'd graduate and be in the summer before college. We'd be competing with plans with her friends for that golden summer period between high school and college. So, summer 2006 was it. (And yes, thoughts of Chevy Chase in the movie, *National Lampoon's Vacation,* did enter my mind.)

My wife and I discussed how to make it work. The initial planning and saving for this started several months before and was purely an adult affair. Fortunately, my wife wasn't working at the time, and I could do my work even while on the road for an extended period. Our goal was to make it an excellent family experience but not end up paying for it for months and years to come by ballooning credit card debt. That worry would take some of the enjoyment out of it for us. It wasn't just the travel and lodging cost; we had a slew of things planned—outings and adventures (rafting, horseback rides, balloon and biplane rides, tours, sightseeing, etc.) we wanted to do along the way that were going to increase the expense. I would have been thinking of the dollars racking up in the debt/credit card column of my mental ledger the entire trip instead of focusing on having fun with my family.

So, my wife and I quietly executed our plan to make sure we could do it under that no-new-debt criteria before we made the announcement. (Nothing would suck more than telling your kids about a great vacation, such as this, and then failing to pull it off.) Months went by, and we were increasingly pleased as it drew closer. Things were working out to pull it off, and it became a treasured, private pleasure as we talked about how our girls would be thrilled when we finally broke the news to them. The gleam in my wife's eyes as she flipped through travel magazines with articles on places we knew we would be seeing relatively soon was especially gratifying to me. It makes me happy to see my family happy.

The real fun started while on spring break vacation that year in Orlando with our daughters when I told them what we were going to do that summer. We all love to travel, and they were ecstatic. I gave them a broad overview of the destinations and asked them to start thinking about some things they wanted to do on the trip. I saw the wheels turning behind their eyes, and soon side discussions were breaking out among them.

When we got back home, I created a countdown calendar, and my two youngest were assigned the duty of marking it off every day. I took my routing- map software and started to rough out the route we'd take. I asked my wife and two oldest daughters, with input from our youngest, to decide particular sights to see and things to do along the way, specifically in those places where we had more than a one-night stay.

Over the next month, they compiled a list. By the end of April, we'd refined the cities and places our route would take us to and what things we'd decided to do that required reservations and booking in advance. My wife handled the two timeshare bookings, sightseeing events, and adventures. I arranged the hotel stays to maximize my Hilton Honors points and further refined the drive time and route so that we only had two hard stretches with a long day of driving. We wanted the vacation to be fun, pleasurable, and not stressed because we exhausted ourselves driving too far for too long on any given day.

The trip was going to take the month of June to the first of July and carry us through twenty states. The travel and time on the road were broken up by overnight stops as needed and in areas where we wanted to spend a day or two to check out nearby sights and scenery.

I've always loved the planning of our vacations. My wife does, too. But this one was heightened by involving our daughters in the process. Each week, the girls talked about the trip and early on started collecting pictures found online of some of the places we'd drive through and those where we'd stay for a while and see. We found shows and documentaries to watch on TV about where we were going and dreamed of when we'd see it for real; we had great conversations while watching them. The anticipation and excitement built as each day they marked off the countdown calendar: from more than two months to one month, to less than thirty days… ten… then five, four, three, two…one!

Finally, *the day* was here. We'd loaded the van the night before. It was fuller than it had ever been, but we had everything we needed for a month on the road far away from home. That morning, everyone got in and at 8:30 I put our new van in reverse and started to back out of the garage...and then stopped, staring straight ahead.

After a half-moment's pause, my wife asked, "Did you forget something?"

I held out for the balance of the moment, and asked, "You girls sure you want to go?"

The van rocked. "Yes... let's go!" And so, we did.

About 312 miles later, I stopped counting after the forty-seventh time the twins had asked, "How far before we stop?" After that first day of driving, they got used to and better tolerated the long drives but looked forward to the stops where we had extended time planned.

Thirty-one days and 7,647 miles later, we pulled back into our garage at home. It felt strange, as I paused for a moment and heard the ticking of the engine.

In that pause, as they all started to get out, I said, "Wait...." Everyone stopped with their doors ajar. "Who wants to do it again?!"

Right now, we're planning its sequel ten years later, The Lowery 2016 Grand Vacation Summer Road Trip II (this includes my wife, of course; my oldest daughter and her new husband; my next oldest and her long-time boyfriend; and the twins, who will be fifteen). And we'll do it the same way with everyone involved in the planning, because I've learned that the best experiences in life are those that you plan for and build up to; that the steps in the journey are just as much fun, or more, than the destination itself.

This story is such an excellent, real-world example that experiences are the cornerstone of a memorable life. Planning them allows you to reconcile ambition, hard work, and sacrifices with living an exciting, enjoyable, and meaningful life. Each step in the process can and should include anticipatory experiences that build to the target *SFL Experience*. Doing this might not be for everyone, and some people might not think they need to plan, or they are lucky and already live their lives this way. But for someone like me, this approach made a dramatic difference in my life—and equally important, for my family, too.

## Important Points to Remember

1. It's not just the event or experience itself; often the buildup, the *anticipation,* can be just as strong in imprinting our experiences as memories.
2. Sometimes, we need to let our primitive mind show us how to use feelings of anticipation and reward to help create positive and fulfilling experiences.
3. We can use this knowledge and purposely create and plan anticipatory events as part of our planning and goal setting to increase the level of happiness in our lives.
4. Build in anticipatory events you look forward to leading up to an SFL Experience to enrich the overall memory and experience.

# PILLAR 3 - CHOICES

*"It is not enough to be busy; so are the ants. The question is: What are we busy about?"*

--Henry David Thoreau

## THE ROLES WE PLAY

I've used as an analogy that your life is really a story created by your direct, personal action or by circumstances and others who you allow to construct it for you. Furthermore, there are characters in stories that play specific roles to move the narrative along; it's like that in life, too. Truly, we can be writers of our life stories. Another way to view it is that you are the director of a movie starring you as the central figure. I'm sure that you know that writers and screenwriters often become directors and wear both hats in creating a film based on their work. And often the director of a movie chooses the cast and the roles the characters' play. That's something that holds true in everyday life, too.

So now we come to the part where we choose our character - our role, or the roles we play, at different times throughout our life. And the decisions we make contribute to our overall life story. These decisions define the experiences we create and enjoy to enhance our lives. These choices become what guide the when, where, and how we implement the *SFL Planning* process.

In my personal life, when I was younger, I didn't take the time to think through how I wanted my life to play out. I hadn't given much thought to the roles I played, or wanted to play, in my own life story. And I certainly didn't think about what I wanted out of each role I played. So while I may have been actively focused on shaping my career, other aspects of my life just happened. Whether it was as a parent, husband, or friend, I wasn't intentionally focusing on forming the type of future I wanted in those roles. I let the future just happen without trying to actively shape it. But I knew there could be more. I had higher expectations for my life in its entirety.

I'm not alone in having that feeling. There is an endless number of people who are successful in a single part of their lives, but unless that is all they care about, they have neglected and risk feeling unfulfilled in the other areas of their lives. I suspect that the gnawing sense of emptiness because of the unsatisfied aspects of their lives is even greater than the feeling of happiness with the parts of their lives that have been successful. They just don't know how to identify, incorporate and manage the other parts of their lives to get the contentment they seek.

The *SFL* approach to planning gives you more

control to live the life you want. By defining the outcomes, you want and purposefully planning the experiences you wish to have in the roles that most matter to you, you create a remarkable future. Thus stated, there's nothing more empowering.

First, let's back up and start at the beginning. You have to first define where you are and where you want to go. Actually, it would be better to ask, which roles do you play now, and which roles do you desire to play in the future?

**The Roles That Matter Most**

We wear many hats in life. It can simply be overwhelming for some (it was for me) to try to wear all of them and do well in all of them at once. For me, it became necessary to identify what life roles I was playing at the time that were most important to me or that I wanted to focus on. When I looked back at my life, it became apparent to me I often did things on auto-pilot mode. I simply didn't think much about the roles I played in my life. Don't get me wrong. I knew I was playing certain roles, but actually thinking about the impact I wanted to have on each, or what I wanted to accomplish in each role, just wasn't happening. I never looked forward to, or back upon, how I was doing or how I was going to make an impact or be better in the various roles I played. I failed to see I needed to purposefully determine what outcomes I wanted and how I was going to achieve them.

I learned early on that I couldn't do everything I wanted equally well. I had to force myself to prioritize and emphasize certain roles, and even certain aspects of the roles, to yield the outcomes I desired. As you go through the process of determining your roles and the areas of your life you wish to focus on, remember, you probably can't do everything you want in life, but you sure can do a whole lot. Just try to make sure the things you do choose to do are the things that will create a happy and contented life.

Determining the roles you play in your life is another linchpin to the *SFL Planning* process. Identifying them will help guide your *SFL Planning* so it is impactful and meaningful to you. These roles can be long-term, possibly lifelong, and include being a spouse, parent, sibling, and a friend. These are traditional, but important roles that you desire and should desire, to create special memories in.

In addition to the lifelong roles, you may also have roles that are more situational, such as being a soccer coach, club leader, homeroom mom, a student, and so on. These roles are more transitional in nature. You get into them, and you get out of them. What you do in-between the beginning and the end is have wonderful and meaningful experiences that create prized memories.

Most people understand the opportunity presented from situational roles–they probably even sought them out. But unfortunately, many don't think about the types of experiences that could boost their happiness and fulfillment while they are in these roles.

Your career and daily responsibilities will also be a source of roles. Whether you are beginning or advancing in your profession, are the owner of your own business or the CEO of your household, many people focus on career progression and accomplishments as a measure of success in their professional life. No doubt it's a good metric if you aspire to grow in your career. However, not enough people focus on gaining the types of experiences along the way that support their career growth; for example, building new skills, getting exposed to different work experiences, and taking on new and different responsibilities.

The secret to being fulfilled in this area of your life is enjoying the journey. Getting a promotion is oftentimes dictated by not only factors you control but also things that you do not, such as business needs and cost constraints. By putting more emphasis on the experiences you have, you will—at a minimum—get more out of the part that is under your control. Actively seeking experiences that you enjoy or are learning about will fuel your motivation as well as help you develop new skills so when the time does come, you are a prepared and engaged candidate.

For the most part, you can and should have roles associated with all three of these areas:

1. Family/friends
2. Situational/transitional
3. Career, profession, daily responsibility

In each area, you should actively plan to grow and create a richer life. Many years ago, when I was in graduate school, I read a phrase in a book that always stuck with me, "You can do anything you want in life, but you can't do everything you want in life." (I know; I'm repeating myself, but this is an important point to remember.) The point is you need to decide on what to focus on, and more importantly, you need to concentrate on the things that will make a difference in the quality of your life.

SFL Planning will help to direct your focus on specific areas of your life so you are able to get the most from those roles, especially those transitional roles that you want to enjoy to their fullest during that time period. By identifying and maintaining focus on those roles that are most meaningful to you, you will be well positioned to create the type of powerful memories that will lead to happiness.

So, what are the roles that deserve *SFL Experiences*? *A deserving role is one that (1) is relevant and meaningful to you, (2) lends itself to experiences that increase happiness, and (3) you want to have memories of.* (Bookmark or highlight this to make it easier to find later. I've italicized it for you here.) After you've read this book thoroughly at least once, return and give this section some serious thought. Remember, you're going to plan experiences that enhance and expand your level of happiness and contentment. Be clear about what roles you want to focus on and what roles you want to have those experiences in. Before going further, I want to expand your thinking on the roles that are important to you. We are often so busy in the here and now that we don't get a chance to think about, and get excited about, the what-if's in life.

## Reinventing Your Future Self

You hear it in many different forms, but it all comes down to a similar point: You either change and improve, or you become stagnant and dull. In a career, it's imperative to continuously learn, to broaden and increase your skills, or you'll discover your promotion path is not that at all…it will become a dead-end. If you are an entrepreneur, you are always scanning your industry, determining the changes and influences affecting the markets you serve and understanding what the competitive landscape looks like. Without that knowledge, you cannot respond and react, and so your business will fail.

In our personal lives, we often strive to get healthier, become fit, and work on developing stable lives. Sometimes that's hard to accomplish when we do what we've always done and get the same results we've always gotten.

But what if we did something else? Something different? What if we decided to reinvent ourselves—that is, create new roles, or focus on new areas of your life? Certainly, you want to stay true to yourself, but what if you stretched the boundaries, experienced new things, and developed more sides of yourself?

You may not regularly participate in social clubs or play golf. But what if you did? How would this change your lifestyle?

If you were not much into participating in charity events, what would be different in your life if you did? Would there be a different circle of acquaintances you would socialize with during those events?

If you don't cook often, taking cooking classes is something that may add a new dimension to your life, one that could not only possibly enhance your dining experience, but be fun as well.

Examine the activities you are currently involved in; what activities could be expanded, or what new things could you try that, as the saying goes, could add some spice to your life? Think about all the new and different experiences you can have in a new role. I encourage you to think about those new and out-of-the-ordinary experiences as you move forward to expand your thinking on what's possible.

We all wish for the ability or the chance for a do-over of certain parts of our lives. But, unfortunately, a functioning time machine has not been created at the time of this writing. The same goes for crystal balls to foresee the future. There aren't any reliable ones out there to my knowledge. But here's something you can do and it is available right now: *Realize that you can shape your own future.*

One way or the other, your future, your life, is going to unfold for better or worse. Why not practice an approach that affords you some control of what happens days, weeks, months, and even years from now? This is an integral part of *SFL Planning*; it describes what we can do today (and tomorrow, etc.) to make that future come true.

## What We Can Learn from Companies that Shape the Future

In the business world, the companies that win in the future are those that invest in the present. That is what leads them to shape the future of their industries. Founded July 5, 1994, Amazon was initially known as an online seller of books. It had an incredible business model that targeted book readers offering better prices and a greater assortment than traditional brick-and-mortar booksellers do. It leveraged technology and the use of the Internet and focused on books that were a safe purchase since you knew what you were getting; you didn't have to feel it out or try it on.

But Amazon was not just another bookseller. It was, quietly at first, transforming the retail industry. It also was not constrained by any ties to past retail business models. It was intent on creating the future of retailing. While it started with selling books, it expanded into other merchandise categories as well as into global markets. And while traditional retailers were chasing Amazon on the Internet, it was continuously changing the rules and tapping new technology as it fit into their vision of serving consumers.

It came out with Amazon Prime, which created a subscription-based model that included free shipping. As retailers were grappling with that free shipping offer that Amazon had as an advantage over their operations, Amazon moved on and was developing actual devices and content. The Amazon Kindle and its offspring are now part of the American consumer landscape.

In other words, Amazon was creating the future of retailing while other retailers were trying to catch up.

Jeff Bezos, Amazon's founder, knew exactly what role he wanted Amazon to play, and is actively shaping the role he wants it to play in the future, to shape the future.

In life, as in business, your success depends on your ability to actively create your future. In most of the important ways, your ability to do so is easier, much easier, than starting a company. Like Amazon, you can benefit from breaking out from the status quo. It's a matter of determining what you want your future to be like and then figuring out the steps you need to take to achieve it.

The future you create should be specific to the roles and areas of your life you want to focus on, but don't be constrained by where you are today and your current roles.

Determining the right roles and corresponding outcomes will lead you down the path you want to go. If you don't take a hand in creating your own future, someone or something else will do it for you.

Make sure you're thinking about your future; about what you need to do to make it turn out the way you want. Either you can be an active creator of what you want, or you can roll the dice and see how things turn out. It's your choice.

## WHAT SHOULD YOU FOCUS ON?

**Identifying Your Roles**

The list of questions that follows will guide you in identifying those most important roles you play today or desire to play in the future that you want to focus on. I recommend taking a blank piece of paper and creating two columns with two headers: Current Roles and Future Roles. As you ask yourself the questions, write your responses in the appropriate column.

Current Roles/Focus Areas of Your Life
- What roles do you play in your life today that are more or less always on (e.g., parent, husband, wife, brother, sister, etc.)? Note: The importance of the role can change and become more or less significant throughout your life. For example, the grandson role may become more important and relevant to his grandmother's life as she becomes older and more dependent as she ages.
- What roles do you play on and off in a given week? Which of these roles are based on certain situations (situation-based roles)?
- Who is important to you? What is your role in that person's life?
- What most matters or should matter to you right now in your life?

Future/Aspirational Roles
- What are the new roles you want to take on or develop in the future?
- Is there a position you want to assume as a member of your community (school, church, charity organizations)?
- Are there career/professional roles that would benefit you (i.e., what are the experiences you want to have to help your professional development)?

Take time to reflect on the questions and your answers as you read and write down your answers. This is the first step in planning using the *SFL* approach.

## WHAT OUTCOMES DO YOU DESIRE?

Once you have identified the roles in your life you want to focus on, determine what you want out of them. For example, if your role is being a parent of a young son, you may feel you haven't spent enough quality time with him. Your wishes are to begin instilling and building character in him in his early years so he has a foundation as he gets older. You might decide you want to spend more time with him to teach him about life lessons and about being responsible. Later, you will decide on specific SFL Experiences that will be fun for both you and your son and support your desired outcome. In other words, the *SFL Experiences* are a means to an end.

The outcomes and objectives you aspire for your roles can vary in both depth and breadth based on what you want to achieve. In this example, in the role of parent, you'll plan experiences that involve plenty of shared quality time. If you are a first-time soccer coach, you will have a different desired outcome and an entirely different set of experiences to support that outcome. In both roles, you will want to have memorable experiences, but will vary based on your role.

To get you thinking about this right now, go ahead and take a different piece of paper and write down just one or two of your roles on the left-hand side of the page. Next to it on the right, think about the type of outcome you desire for each role. Take a few minutes and reflect on this. Your desired outcome could be based on a feeling that you had before that has been missing lately. Or, it may be an altogether new dimension to an ongoing relationship. Either way, what you desire should have an element of emotion and depth. Write it down next to your role and we'll come back to this a little later and build upon it.

Sometimes it's easier to understand concepts using examples. In the chapter titled, *SFL in Action*, I go through three examples which may help you get your head around the concepts and how to think through the process.

## Your Perspective Determines Your Outcomes

Some people are naturally good at planning experiences for the roles and areas of their lives that most matters, whether they do it purposefully or unknowingly. My own experience is that it takes specific intent and thoughtfulness to determine what you want to happen in the areas of your life that are most important to you. This takes a perspective on the big picture of your life: your past, present, and what you envision for the future. And it's personal. Only you know what experience-based outcomes you want. What you focus on is up to you. Just know that you can do anything, but you can't do everything you want (at least not all at once). Again, keep things in perspective.

## Making Your Roles Memorable

The real power of *SFL Planning* comes when you incorporate *SFL Experience*s into your roles. You want to create those experiences that you want to remember, cherish, and retell in the areas of your life that matter most.

Remember that memories are the glue that holds your life together and provide a solid foundation for everything that happens and will happen. Everything you learned, your personality and how you behave, are all influenced by the experiences in your life. Without memorable experiences, well, you'll have an unmemorable life.

To sum up, for each of your roles, your objective is to determine what outcome you desire for it. Once you have done that, you shift and identify *SFL Experiences* that support that outcome. I've summarized the *SFL Experience* characteristics described previously in the following section.

**Make Them Physically Active in Nature:** *SFL Experience*s have an element of play and motion. The more play, the more neurotransmitters are released in your body and brain. And, by the way, you can be perfectly horrible at doing something—it doesn't matter. The key is to accept and realize it's okay, and often healthy, to make fun and laugh at yourself. Remember to always seek perspective in life. You can't get it sitting still or remaining alone. It's that perspective that helps give your experiences more breadth and depth.

**Make Your Experiences Stand Out:** The experiences you choose to have should be unique, different, out of the ordinary, and possibly a bit uncomfortable. Get out of your comfort zone and try something different and exceptional. And the more unusual or unexpected they are, the better—they will stand out even more. Even when the experience doesn't go as expected, its distinctive nature means there will still be a story to remember, tell, and retell.

**Share Your Experiences:** To be exceptionally memorable, you need to share your experiences with other people. You may think you are an introvert, and you very well may be, but to get the most enjoyment out of an experience, even an introvert needs to act more like an extrovert and share the experience with others.

**Make Them Personally Meaningful and Fun:** Your experiences should align with who you are and what you want to get done in your life. That's the essence of what you want them to be about. Remember, it's exciting to explore, so don't shortchange yourself by limiting yourself. You may be pleasantly surprised by discovering new dimensions of yourself as a person.

These are the characteristics of experiences that can increase your happiness and well-being. Plan them and create your life stories.

You previously identified a role in your life and a corresponding outcome and wrote it down on a piece of paper. Look back at that now and see if you can envision an experience or multiple experiences that would support this outcome. Remember, think of something that has the characteristics of an *SFL Experience* that we just described. Write down a few ideas on the paper next to your role and desired outcome.

You might think about experiences and events you've had in the past that you enjoyed doing but haven't done in a while. And that's okay; what you want to steer away from is the routine. Going to your favorite restaurant on a Friday night may be a pleasurable experience. Who doesn't want an occasional break from cooking and cleaning? But if you do it every Friday night, it's not going to stand out. This is the time to think freely about ideas that are different from the norm and by their very nature are enjoyable and stimulating. You may come up with multiple experiences. *Great*; the more, the better!

Once you have identified the target *SFL Experience*(s), the next step is figuring out when you want them to take place. It's not enough to write down the experience you want—that is just a hope and a wish. To make it tangible, something you can achieve, you're going to have to make it *actionable*.

Setting a timeframe of when you want to have those experiences gives it legs and makes it real. Making your experience actionable will make your plan achievable. Write down when you want the experience to take place next to the *SFL Experience* you identified previously. Depending on what it is, you could put down a particular date, month, or even year. Don't worry if you can't be exact right now. Later in the process, you'll have a chance to better clarify and get more specific about the timing of the experience.

The important thing is that by placing a timing around the experience(s), you begin to add an explicit dimension to what these experiences represent: a chapter in your life story you are about to write. And that in itself is exciting.

For ideas, examples, and a walkthrough of this process, see the following *SFL In Action* section, which bring this process to life.

**Important Points to Remember**

1. In our lives, we intentionally and sometimes inadvertently take on many roles. These roles directly and indirectly mold us and shape our experiences. We must take a hands-on active approach to defining the roles that will result in the type of experiences we want in life.
2. Equally important is our perspective on those roles throughout life. Perspectives dictate what and how the story unfolds, so it's important to form the right perspective to accomplish the outcomes we desire in life.
3. Realize you can shape your own future by expanding and identifying different roles you want to play or areas you want to focus on. Expanding your horizons will unlock variety in your life and a

multitude of new experiences. Remember, variety is the spice of life.

4. Knowing what you desire out of the roles that most matter will guide you in determining the *SFL Experiences* to have. Plan them so they support your desired outcomes for each role you want to focus on in your life.
5. Make your SFL Plan real and achievable by setting a timeframe to when you want the *SFL Experiences* to take place.

# SFL IN ACTION

# MAKING IT REAL

*"If you are waiting each morning for happiness to come your way you will only wake up and fall asleep miserable. Happiness must be made not found."*

--Unknown

The following examples bring *SFL Planning* to life. They are meant to highlight, not only the key SFL concepts, but also how those concepts are used within the context of life planning. In the scenarios, note the importance of determining what was missing or desired by the protagonist in an important area of their life. The desired outcomes are often the result of a longing that is personal and meaningful. That's a good place to start when you are reflecting on your roles and desired outcomes when you start planning your *SFL Experiences*.

### EXAMPLE 1 - ANGELA

**Role:** Mom

Angela had been spending a lot of time working a few extra hours at home in addition to her usual part-time office job as a corporate lawyer. She was also the "CEO of the Household, Inc." as she called it. During weekdays, she moonlighted as the taxi extraordinaire, taking her daughters, aged fourteen and sixteen, to a myriad of different after-school activities. On weekends, that didn't stop. And while her husband helped out, the activities of the two girls would usually take them in different directions. She would take one daughter one way and her husband would take the other daughter another way. While generally a happy and close family, **Angela was missing her family time** and wanted something her family could do together, real bonding moments that a too hectic life was depriving her of as she lived each day reacting to the moment and the responsibilities of a career and homemaker. As a mother, she wanted to create a greater "we are family" feeling that had been lost in the hustle of the day-to-day, week-to-week activities. She wanted to do something healthy, wholesome, and challenging together as a family. The opportunity to create that feeling was *what Angela desired for her role*.

Angela and her husband thought about it. They shared their idea with their daughters and discussed it together with each family member providing ideas. Since they were all avid runners, they thought doing something involving running or hiking would be easy to rally around. They ultimately decided that running a ten-mile race would give the whole family an ambitious goal. They usually stuck to running a three- to four-mile distance, and this would be a challenge, as a family, they would need to rise to. It also gave them a purpose when they exercised, and they decided they would do longer runs together on Sundays. They looked at different races in their local area and found the Broad Street Run in Philadelphia. It was a fun, ten-mile race that was four months away, which would give them plenty of time to train for the event.

As the family looked into the race and the activities surrounding it, they saw that it was often run by teams of individuals who ran for charities. They thought it would be a great idea to run for the Make-A-Wish Foundation, which gave them an extra incentive (helping others) to rally around as part of this experience.

Angela became the organizer of the "Jones Family Summer Rally" event and laid out the essential activities that needed to get done as part of the family's summer event. She thought of the following milestones that became their mini-events they can look forward as they prepared for the run:

- Sign up for the race (i.e. make the commitment).
- Ask some of their family and friends to sponsor them (i.e., donate to the charity). Although she wanted to make sure her family didn't feel this was a "beg-a-thon event," she wanted everyone to feel it was something they would be willing to do.

- Create a training schedule for the family.
- One of their daughters suggested creating a training-music playlist that would include some individual favorites but also some shared family ones. This further solidified that "we are family" feeling (and yes, "We Are Family" was definitely one of the songs on the playlist).
- Dad suggested finding a restaurant near the finish line of the race where they could have post-run lunch after they had completed the race and celebrate their family accomplishment.

**What Actually Happened**

As in life, and as you follow the *SFL* approach to planning, there are some twists and turns—usually for the better. New ideas pop up as you think about how you can look forward to something. An anticipatory mindset unleashes a creativity that fosters fun and playfulness.

Angela wanted to create something that could be an extraordinary memory of the Jones Family Summer Rally. She thought a rubber wristband with the words, "Good Alone, But Better Together," portrayed the sentiment she wanted her family to feel. She had them made up and gave them to her daughters and husband as something they all would wear as they trained and ran the race.

The family read wonderful stories and found out more about the Make-A-Wish Foundation and the great work that it did for children and their families. Reassured that it was a worthwhile cause, and while they weren't pushy, they asked their family and friends to sponsor them. While their original intention was to just help raise money for the charity, they discovered their friends not only were willing to donate money but also loved the idea of running in the race as well and decided to join them. The potential grew for the event to become an even larger experience for the family by having so many connections also involved in the event. Given the additional family and friends who were joining the race, Dad thought it was better to reserve a larger outdoor seating area for all them to go to after the race to share their stories. The anticipation for what was planned for after the event added to the excitement as they trained for the run.

While each person in the Jones's family was free to train however and whenever he or she wanted during the week, given scheduling challenges (Dad liked to run in the morning, Mom during the day, and the daughters after school), they had decided that Sunday would include the longer runs that were part of the training regimen to finish a ten-miler. And they would do those runs together (or at least start together but finish at their individual pace). This would give them an opportunity to talk about their individual training as well as the upcoming event in general. And one of the daughters thought it would be a great idea to take plenty of pictures during the training runs as memories of the times the family was together as they prepared for the event.

During the runs, the family decided on the prerace dinner meal and prerace breakfast menu. They thought it would be best to keep to the traditional meals, which included carb loading. So, the menu was set: spaghetti and garlic rolls for dinner, and bagels and pancakes for breakfast.

Angela and her daughters decided it was important to get foot massages and new race gear as part of the prerace activities. They planned a shopping day specifically for buying new running clothes, and, of course, made appointments for foot and back massages while out doing their shopping. Dad decided he liked his old ("I'm used to them") workout clothes and shoes, and while a foot massage was tempting, he thought he would rather have one after the race. The activities before the race became events for the whole family, and pictures, even silly ones, were taken to commemorate all that they did together.

The day before the race, they all went to get their race bib numbers—918, 919, 920, and 921—and their race chips that would be used to track their times. This was a big moment, and not just because of all the effort they had put into getting to this point, but because they were joined by thousands of others who were as excited about the race as they were. The energy and buzz were uplifting for them. The prerace dinner was at an Italian restaurant that Dad had picked and made reservations specifically for this day. It was as planned—spaghetti and garlic rolls on every plate (Dad had some meatballs, too). And of course, more pictures were taken.

Race day morning finally came. Angela had been waiting for this moment as she prepared the bagel and pancake breakfast. She felt proud of how the family had come together around this race. But maybe more importantly, she knew how the family had bonded had created wonderful memories, and not just for today. There were so many stories along the way that would last forever. The food was ready, and Angela could not help herself. It was still early, but time to get them rolling. She played "We are Family" on high volume to wake the rest of her family.

At the race, they took a final picture of the family at the starting line: all the ladies in their fashionable race day gear; Dad in his old shorts, shirt, and sneakers, but looking just like Dad wanted to look. With a joint, "See you at the finish line," they were off with a thousand other runners.

Following the race, the family got together with a few other friends at the restaurant. There were lots of stories of the run told during brunch. Dad was eating enough to gain back all the weight he had lost during his training (an extra bonus). Lots of pictures and videos were taken leading up to the race and at the race. And the weekend, after the race the family got together to see their video scrapbook and relive their favorite moments. They all loved the experience so much, they decided to train for an upcoming half-marathon.

This is an example of how a memorable *SFL Experience* can be extended to be so much richer. Thinking about and planning the right anticipation-building stepping stones can lead to a treasure trove of memories, even before the targeted *SFL Experience* is achieved.

## EXAMPLE 2 - JAKE

**Role:** Husband

Jake wanted to share more time with his wife. He had been busy establishing his start-up, e-commerce business and felt distanced from his wife, Liz. His conversations with her always centered around the kids' school, bills, mortgages, house chores, and, of course, the business.

He reflected on this and **wanted more quality time with his wife and to gain back some "our time"** with her and create personally shared moments. He thought if the two of them could share a special event, it would give them a chance to spend time on something that wasn't about finances or the business.

Jake talked to his wife about it. They had close friends, but since everyone was busy with their own lives, they hadn't had a chance to spend much time with them. They thought it would be fun to host a dinner party at their home where they could invite friends they hadn't seen in a while. That event would be a target *SFL* Experience.

They thought through what they wanted to do and came up with stepping stones they could do together that would lead up to the event. These anticipatory events were the following:

- Take cooking classes together on the weekend. They both enjoyed cooking and thought it would be something fun they could do together and also learn to make new recipes they could use for their dinner party.
- Selecting the main entrée as well the appetizers and dessert dishes, which included researching recipes they thought they and their friends would enjoy.
- A planned practice dinner a month before the big dinner party to work out any kinks and to make sure they knew how to make all the new dishes.

- Leading up to the practice dinner and before the actual dinner party, they selected music for the evening that captured the essence of the evening.

## What Actually Happened

Jake and Liz saw that Cinco de Mayo was a couple of months away and thought they could have a fun night with their friends with a Mexican theme. It was far enough away that they could do all the planning and preparation together. It would help them be ready to create a delicious meal for their friends and spend some quality time together doing something new.

Liz started looking for some good Mexican dishes and Jake immediately took on bartending duties and jumped into researching drink recipes. He planned to set up a Margarita bar and selected glasses that they would give to their guests to take home with them as a memento of the occasion. Together, they planned the nachos and tacos stations where they and their guests would prepare appetizers and finger foods. They both loved the idea of having as a main entrée chicken with Mole sauce with rice and beans. Jake thought they should have guacamole and chips as well. He thought it would be fun to get some of their guests involved by having them help prepare the guacamole that evening. The guacamole would be as fresh as possible, and they'd also have some fun. For the nachos and guacamole, they decided to make homemade chips rather than buy them at the store. That was also something they could learn how to make together.

Liz and Jake had a lot of fun learning about and listening to classic Mexican songs as they put together a playlist for the evening. They particularly liked learning about Mariachi music and included a massive dose of that Mexican folk music in their playlist.

The most fun was practicing making their dishes, but they realized it was a lot of food. They decided to keep the chicken with Mole sauce as the main entrée, and stick to homemade chips and guacamole as their appetizer, but not include the tacos. Even though it was not authentic Mexican, but to keep things simple, they decided to serve ice cream for dessert with a variety of toppings the guests could choose from.

The night of the dinner was wonderfully entertaining. Jake was very proud of his Margarita bar and the knowledge he had of each variation of the mixed drink.

The guests were more than happy to roll up their sleeves and help out with the guacamole. Everyone got into the spirit of the evening, especially with the Mariachi music playing in the background.

Jake took pictures and videos leading up to and during their Mexican Fiesta Night. He couldn't wait to pull it all together for some reminiscing with this wife.

It didn't take long after watching the video scrapbook that Jake and Liz were already thinking about "Little Italy Night."

The week leading up to "Mexican Fiesta Night" looked like this:

| | |
|---:|:---|
| Saturday: | Jake purchased the Margarita ingredients for the different recipes. (That night, both Jake and Liz took part in trying out a couple.) They confirmed the music playlist (which they played as they tried some of the Margarita recipes). |
| Sunday: | Jake and Liz went to the market to buy decorations, recipe ingredients, and all the other beverages. |
| Mon – Thur: | Liz confirmed the party guest list. |
| Friday: | Got ahead by preparing certain foods, such as cutting up the tortillas for the homemade nacho chips. Decorate the house with a festive Mexican theme. |
| Saturday: | Have fun! |

## EXAMPLE 3 - RICHARD

**Role:** Son of Aging Parent

Richard knew he was in the twilight of his time with his father, who was seventy-five years old. **He wanted to have a final once-in-a-lifetime experience with his dad** in appreciation for all he'd done and meant to him while his father could still get around easily.

He thought he could take a cross-country trip with his dad going to various major league baseball games. His father loved baseball and had instilled this love in him. Richard always remembered the baseball games he had gone to with his dad when he was younger. Taking his father with him to see baseball games in different cities would be an excellent memory for both of them while his father still had a few good years left.

In talking with his dad, who thought it was an unbelievable idea. They both thought rather than doing a cross-country trip, they could target the Northeast and Mid-Atlantic areas. The New York teams, Boston Red Sox, Philadelphia Phillies, Baltimore Orioles, and Washington Nationals all played in the region. They would have many opportunities across the cities to get plenty of baseball games in. And the travel would be easy enough so they could spend time doing other things and visiting other great sports venues and sights, including sports bars and doing the *Rocky* steps together, albeit slowly, in Philadelphia.

Richard and his father spent lots of time together thinking through some of the things they had to do in preparation. Even planning the activities they wanted to do on the trip was an exciting thing that drew them even closer together. They decided to cheer for the home team in each city and buy shirts and caps for each game as part of their road trip souvenirs.

Some of the *Stepping Stones* they did together, which became fun activities in and of themselves, included the following:

- Researched the schedule to see what were the most games they could go to in the different cities.
- Researched other sites they wanted to see in each of the towns they were going to, including well-known historical sports bars.
- Ordered their souvenir shirts and caps for each game they were going to attend.
- Researched local radio stations for each home team to listen to some of the local shows on the Internet to hear what the local buzz was for the team. This was Richard's father's suggestion and activity, and he shared the news with his son in daily phone calls leading up to their road trip.

This way, each of them felt more like a "local" as they cheered for the home team in each city.

**What Actually Happened**

Richard decided he would take a week off from work, leaving two weekends and the in-between week for the road trip with his dad, although he wanted to look at the baseball schedules before deciding which week to take off. Richard and his father went online to see the baseball schedules for all the teams in the Northeast and Mid-Atlantic areas. They found there was one week where they could go to five different baseball games in four cities and still have time to enjoy the city.

They researched and called friends who were in a couple of the cities they were going to visit and asked for recommendations of places to go; this would also give them a chance to reconnect and hang out with old friends. They loved the idea of eating at favorite local restaurants, including Italian restaurants in the North End of Boston, eating Philly Cheese Steak sandwiches in Philadelphia, and eating anything and everything in New York City. They both had fun choosing restaurants to go to in each of the cities both before the game and after.

They took many pictures and videos along the way, of course. Richard took pictures of the tickets and the local newspaper's sports section and baseball team as part of the scrapbook. More pictures were taken when they met up with family and friends along the way. Richard heard many stories he had never heard about his father from some of his dad's friends. Through those stories and the eyes and voices of his father's friends, he got to know his father in a new and different way he would have never had, except for this special trip. Richard saw his father laugh as many of those stories were told. They visited many tourist sites, and it was classic watching his dad climb the *Rocky* steps and throw his arms up in the air, reenacting the scene from the movie. The baseball games were memorable as well and they immensely enjoyed cheering for the home team as if they were local fans.

While the trip was one Richard will always cherish, the favorite part of it all for Richard was that his dad always told stories about it every time he went somewhere and met someone. Richard will forever have many memories with his father to share, but he was especially proud of how the road trip made his father feel and the stories he would always tell about it. It meant so much to Richard to know he had done this for his father; it had obviously been a tremendously happy time for this father, and something Richard had equally enjoyed as well.

**Important Points to Remember**

1. These scenarios of *SFL Planning* in action are representative of what experiences can be intertwined with your specific roles in life to make your life more memorable and meaningful.
2. Coming up with a desired outcome, *SFL Experience*s, and stepping stones you look forward to are all part of the memory you make. Make your life story remarkably memorable for you and others.
3. What actually happens is often not exactly as originally planned. And that's okay. What actually happens is sometimes even more memorable and fun than initially planned. The most important lesson is to enjoy the journey and make those memories along the way.

# MAKING SFL PLANNING PART OF YOUR LIFE

# THE PLANNING SYSTEM

*"The road leading to a goal does not separate you from the destination; it is essentially a part of it."*

--Charles De Lint

The *SFL Planning System* enables you to plan the experiences and activities necessary to reach higher levels of happiness in the areas of your life that matter to you. It isn't common to plan this way. We spend much of our time crossing items off our checklists and not enough time doing the things that add happiness to our lives. Being productive is needed to be successful in the business of life, but crossing items off your task list does not, in itself, lead to long-term happiness.

Knowing the outcomes and experiences we want to have is an important part of creating our future. Equally vital is identifying and planning what we need to do to make those experiences happen. This is where the execution of our plan comes into play.

An essential element to making and keeping *SFL Planning* as part of your life is to make it a regular habit – part of your daily routine. I know that's easier said than done, but it helps when you have a process to follow (what to do) that is supported by tools and a framework you use to help you execute the process. And, of course, you also have to have the right knowledge on how to do it. Having all three of those in place will make it considerably easier to establish a repeatable habit. You'll be fighting uphill if they are not in place and it's likely you'll have limited or no success in bringing about the changes you want. Change is inherently challenging so you want to give yourself every chance to improve your odds to be successful.

I've described the *SFL Planning* principles and concepts in the preceding parts of this book. I'm now going to describe a system you can follow to make *SFL Planning* work for you. In the beginning, it may feel forced or unnatural, but as you continue to use it, it will become second nature and, hopefully, will become part of a regular routine.

## THE SYSTEM

I'm a practical person. I know my strengths and my weaknesses, what works for me, and what doesn't. Fascinated by planners, I use them often to record my long-term goals as well as to organize my weekly and daily checklists. I've also been an avid follower of different principles and methods behind many of the planning systems available. The problem with many of the planning systems is this: oftentimes, once you identify a long-term goal, you end up putting it into a master to-do list that has no timetable or reasonable intermediate steps accompanying it. Or alternatively, a goal is plopped on a future date in the calendar where we lose sight of it and tend to forget it's even there because we too easily switch our focus to the daily grind.

A big reason I believe most people fail in reaching their goals is that they do not lay out a clear path to achieving them. It's like driving to a city you've never been to before, but you don't look at the map to see what the precise route is to get you there. You tell yourself, "It's north and east of here…" And so, you set off in that general direction. Maybe you'll eventually get there or at least in the vicinity. More than likely, though, you won't; this is almost certainly to be the case for destinations of a greater distance.

There is no shortage of available material on setting goals and probably even more on managing checklists. I realized, however, there was not much out there that dealt with the linking of long-term goals and outcomes to medium- and shorter-term steps. There is a seminal business book called the *Balanced Scorecard* by Robert Kaplan and David Norton. It is popular in the business world because it provides a performance management framework that helps executives keep track of activities that link inputs, processes, and outcomes. It focuses on the importance of monitoring and managing these components to achieve strategic objectives. In other words, the framework is used to control the medium- and short-term activities—

*Stepping Stones*—needed to reach a longer-term strategic result. Likewise, the *SFL* approach to planning is a refined and personal approach to achieving your long-term desired outcomes.

The *SFL Planning System* provides the framework to enable better life planning in the areas that matter to you. Much like a business executive might use the *Balanced Scorecard* approach to achieve their strategic outcomes, you link your intermediate *Stepping Stones* to your desired longer-term *SFL Experience*.

## If-Then Planning

In execution, the *SFL Planning System* links multiple planning horizons, in other words, shorter-term activities are planned that naturally lead you to your longer-term result. Simply stated, it uses an If-Then model. In other words, "If you do $X$, then $Y$ will happen." This approach is crucial as many personal planning systems do not emphasize these shorter-term activities nearly enough, if at all, which enable you to make and have confidence in a plan that leads to your objective – which, in our case, is our *SFL Experience.*

The combination of planning *SFL Experiences* using an If-Then model is effective and powerful in increasing your overall happiness. The benefits of an If-Then approach to planning and linking short-term actions are numerous. Some are listed below:

- Each action leads to the next action or builds on the previous action.
- It's your gauge on how you are doing toward reaching your ultimate experience; that is, if you don't do X then you may not be reaching Y.
- Gives you clarity on the steps you need to take to get to your destination rather than just "head north and east…"
- Keeps your target *SFL Experience* on your radar and in view.
- And most significantly, you can turn the short-term steps into mini-experiences themselves to create a series of positive and exciting events you look forward to.

I'll give you some personal perspective on this. Here are some goals I have set out for myself in the past before developing the *SFL Planning System*:

- Lose ten pounds
- Develop a retirement plan
- Achieve work/life balance
- Run a marathon
- Get more involved with charitable organizations

I know. Most of these are examples you could

find on anyone's list of objectives or take from countless New Year's resolutions. And, yes, some are vague, unmeasurable and not action-oriented. Nevertheless, most of these goals were what I thought I wanted at the time. Some I even achieved although I never put them in the context of the roles I played at the time. The difference in why I achieved some of these goals and not others was that I had a plan – actual steps and milestones, that I followed to help me achieve the goals I did. An example of this is my goal to run a marathon. This is a good example that demonstrates and makes real—and obvious, the importance of linking shorter-term, intermediate steps to the longer-term result (If-Then).

**Breaking Down My Goal to Run a Marathon**

To run and finish a marathon is not something you can just get up and do. You (at least most of us) need a training plan. In other words, you need to chart your course. Achieving the goal of running a marathon starts by first picking one to run. Usually, that entails a definite date as most marathons are held annually.

In my case, it was the 2002 Chicago Marathon which took place in October. You have to sign up way in advance for the marathon as it fills up quickly. If I tried to sign up in September, one month before the marathon, I would have been told there were no more entries available. Sure, I could have run it as a bandit (someone who runs a race without an official entry), but that meant I would not have been recognized officially. And if I was going to run 26.2 miles, someone had better officially record that! The reality is, if you wish to run in the Chicago Marathon legitimately, you have to sign up months ahead, and that requires planning. Once signed up, if you are from out of town, you will need to make all the travel arrangements - including the hotel and flight arrangements, if driving is out of the question. If you wait too long, the hotels near the marathon will be all booked, and the flights become very expensive. You get the picture.

Then, of course, there is the training. For someone who typically maxed out at 3-milers, being able to run 26.2 miles is a very big leap and would require a much greater and more intense level of training. I'm talking months of preparation, and forget about actually being competitive; that's just for being able to finish the marathon. For me, getting a relatively fast time was not the goal, but I was very intent on starting and finishing the marathon. I won't lie to you; the training was brutal for me. But I stuck to a training plan published by Hal Higdon, which laid out a day-by-day training program. Hal Higdon is one of the founders of the Road Runners Club of America and a prolific writer on the topic of running, including marathon training. And the training got me to the point where I could actually line up at the starting line next to my wife (my girlfriend at the time) and believe I can finish the marathon. A few hours later—okay, quite a few hours later—I'm proud to say, I crossed the finish line.

So, while running and finishing the marathon was an experience I aspired to have, I couldn't simply get off the couch and do it. By the very nature of the goal I set, I needed to take very specific forward-looking actions in order to prepare for the marathon.

In many ways, running the Chicago Marathon was an *SFL Experience* even though I didn't consider it this way at the time. It was physical in nature, shared, personally meaningful, and unique. It became the "I Will Cross the Chicago Marathon Finish Line in October 2002" experiential goal. That was the target *SFL Experience*. But there were many intermediate steps—the *Stepping Stones*—I needed to accomplish to have a hope of reaching my objective. For example, in the training program I followed, long runs were crucial for building up my endurance and were added to the training plan. They were essentially the *Stepping Stones* to being trained and ready for running the marathon. Candidly, when I first saw the training program, "long runs" of ten miles in week five, fifteen miles in week ten, and twenty miles in week fifteen were daunting to someone who was basically exhausted after just a three mile jog. But those

Stepping Stones eventually became experiences to celebrate in themselves as they were meaningful, albeit tiring, victories. They were made possible by the continued progression of accomplishing even smaller goals: my daily and weekly runs.

This was a good example of the If-Then model in action. There was a clear itinerary for me from being able to run just three miles in the very beginning of my journey to where I could finish a 26.2-mile marathon. There were several experiences accumulated along the way, culminating with crossing that finish line in Chicago. I still vividly remember when I first saw the finish line ahead of me. Though warm and sweaty from the run, I got chills throughout my body when I knew I was actually going to cross it. By the end of the journey, I had created many memories—admittedly some that were painful but equally memorable—that became part of my life story.

Think about the journey: a series of decisions and steps I needed to take, including the initial one to decide to run a marathon. That was my target *SFL Experience,* to accomplish something significant (for me at least) that was also healthy and notable—a memory of an accomplishment that would last my lifetime. It bears repeating:

*Many goals are unachievable because there isn't a clear understanding of how they will be achieved.*

But if you break them down into smaller goals and *Stepping Stones*, you can achieve almost anything. While my story about running the marathon, and having the experiences that led to it aligned with the *SFL* approach, at the time, I wasn't thinking about it that way. But identifying the goal that was the target experience and then determining the plan that helped me run and finish the marathon is a perfect, albeit accidental, alignment with the *SFL Planning System*. It became an exciting and personally meaningful chapter in my life story. It was only later that I incorporated the importance of roles and anticipation as part of the overall approach for *SFL Planning*.

Reflections, based not only on this experience but also others in my life, led to research that became a core reason why the *SFL* approach to planning works. I learned that to achieve my long-term outcomes, it helped to reverse-plan goals and determine intermediate *Stepping Stones* required to get there.

These intermediate *Stepping Stones* created additional memories and developed that pleasurable sense of anticipation (itself a memory-creating emotion) you want threaded throughout your entire life. Many people think about the ultimate outcome, but unless there is a plan on how to get there, you're relying on hope and dreams only. A concrete plan with defined steps and excitement built in will get you where you want to go.

**Important Points to Remember**

1. To achieve long-term goals, use an If-Then approach to planning. Reverse plan and determine the intermediate steps needed to reach your ultimate outcome.
2. The lack of intermediate steps and milestones which link short-term activities to longer-term goals is a big reason why results are not consistently achieved.
3. There are a number of benefits to adding and linking shorter-term activities to longer-term goals. The most meaningful is turning the short-term stepping stones into mini *SFL Experiences* themselves to build anticipation and enrich your memories.

# WRITING YOUR LIFE STORY

*"People with goals succeed because they know where they're going."*

--Earl Nightingale

As I mentioned previously, the *SFL Planning System* uses an If-Then method to planning. Linking intermediate *Stepping Stones* to your target *SFL Experience* in effect creates a roadmap to the memories you wish to have as part of your overall *SFL Experience*. One of the most effective ways to create your roadmap is to work backward (reverse plan) from your desired target *SFL Experience* and think through the events and activities that will lead to what you want to achieve.

However, before we start linking *Stepping Stones* to *SFL Experiences* we first need to make sure we're focusing our efforts in the right place. The *SFL Planning* process starts with identifying the roles that matter to you most and determining your desired outcomes so that's where we will begin.

# The Process

Following below is a series of steps that outlines the *SFL Planning System* process. It uses questions to guide your thinking for each step. The questions are there to provoke and help you think through the outputs for each step in the *SFL Planning System* process, but don't think these are the only questions. They are, however, meant to provoke your thinking and provide you direction on how to think about your responses. The steps of the process build on each other so take the time to begin with the first step and work through each subsequent step.

It may help to write the responses from each step on paper (or electronically). I recommend you use your planner to help organize the outputs and to make them real. There are also templates of planning pages I personally use that you can download from the SetForLifeExperiences.com website.

## Step 1: Identify the Role(s) You Want to Focus on and the Desired Outcome(s)

1. What are the critical roles you play in your life today?
2. What matters most to you?
3. What do you want to focus on the most?
4. What future roles do you foresee for yourself?

5. What roles in your life today do you want to add some excitement to?
6. What outcome do you desire from this role or area of focus; that is, what's missing or what do you want more of?
7. What outcome, if achieved, can meaningfully and positively impact this role?

**Helpful Tips:**

- Write down the answers to these questions in a planner or somewhere you can revisit on a regular basis and are able to reflect on them periodically (e.g. monthly).
- Don't limit yourself to one desired outcome for each role at this time. Approach this from different angles so you have more–and possibly better–ideas to choose from. Often, it's the third or fourth idea you get that really gets you excited. Remember, an important part of creating a happy life is understanding that different times and circumstances require us to adapt and be flexible. More ideas will present more options that might work better for you during those different times.
- Remember, you can do anything you want in life, but you can't do everything you want. When assessing the roles and outcomes you want to enjoy SFL Experiences in, make sure you pick those that are most important to you at the time.

- Your role can be situational and relevant now, or could be one in the future. You may want to go through this process when you take on a new situational role. Situational roles add rich dimensions to your life story. Actively seek them out to add zest to your life and to create your future.

## Step 2: Determine What SFL Experience(s) You Wish to Have for Each Role

1. What experiences would help you achieve the outcome you desire for this role or area of focus?
2. Does the experience involve physical action?
3. What experiences would be different and stand out from your everyday life?
4. Would these experiences make good stories to remember and share?
5. Does the experience align with who you are and what you want from your life?
6. Can you experience it with others; that is, who would you involve in this experience that would enhance its enjoyment (and make it more memorable)?

### Helpful Tips:

- Think fun and playful; something you can easily look forward to.

- Look for opportunities that combine as many of the *SFL Experience* characteristics as possible.
- Many times, when we think of sharing an experience, we think in terms of only two people, but including others in the experience is another way to boost your happiness.
- Go through this step periodically so you keep things fresh.

## Step 3: Determine When You Want to Have the SFL Experience

1. For each *SFL Experience* you previously identified, when do you want to have the experience? Write down the year, month, or week you would like next to each one you have listed.
2. Does the *SFL Experience* align with specific important dates for example: birthdays, holidays, events? Can it?
3. Do you need to plan/schedule around other events or conflicts during this time frame, and if so, how will you make yourself available?
4. Write down any additional planning considerations next to each *SFL Experience*, e.g. the schedules of the other people who are part of the experience.

**Helpful Tips:**

- When identifying the timing of an *SFL Experience,* look for local or other established events you can make part of it. Charity, sporting, and other entertaining venues are a great way to enjoy and enrich an *SFL Experience.*
- *SFL Experience*s can be in the near-term (tomorrow) or can be far in the future (years away). The intermediate *Stepping Stones* will bridge the gap between your present and future goal(s).

## Step 4: Use Stepping Stones to Build Anticipation

1. What events and activities can you can look forward to that lead up to your target SFL Experience?
2. Are there prerequisite or preparation activities you can do with others that lead up to your experience? Are there topics to learn about or historical background you can learn together related to the SFL Experience?
3. Can you create a music playlist that captures the mood and spirit of the SFL Experience?
4. Will there be a post SFL Experience event that can extend the overall memory of the experience?
5. When do you want the stepping stones to take place? Determine what month or quarter they

should take place and write them down.
7. If you can be specific, determine the week or even the day the stepping stones are to take place and schedule them in your planner.

**Helpful Tips:**

- Work backward and think through exciting or enjoyable mini-experiences you can anticipate on the way to your future goal.
- Be creative when you're thinking about the stepping stones.
- Engaging your emotions is helpful in determining the types of stepping stones to incorporate into your plan. An effective way to do this is to visualize those events that create anticipation.
- The more the stepping stones exhibit the four qualities of an *SFL* Experience (i.e., physical/active, unique, shared, personally meaningful/fun), the more memorable they will be.
- Having dates makes them real so put a date where you can. You can use these dates to track them on a monthly and weekly basis.
- Musical playlists are great for reliving your *SFL Experience*, especially if you use it as background music to a video or photo slideshow.

At this point, you have completed the first level of

*SFL Planning*: You identified the roles you want to focus on, the key outcomes you desire for each role, identified *SFL Experiences* which support each outcome and added a timeframe to each of them. You've also thought through some *Stepping Stones* to create excitement and anticipation to further enrich the overall experience and put timeframes around those.

This is typically the most enjoyable and inspirational part of planning. You get to be reflective, ambitious, and aspirational. You have a vision that motivates you and you look forward to. Unfortunately, this is often when most people stop planning and never reach what they envisioned. In the next section, I'll review how make it happen.

# LIVING YOUR LIFE STORY

*"A goal without a plan is just a wish."*

--Larry Elder

In this chapter, you'll switch from vision planning to execution planning. You'll learn about the monthly, weekly, and daily planning processes you can follow to help you execute your plan. This is where it all becomes real in your life. Without action at this level, the *SFL Experiences* and *Stepping Stones* you desire are simply words on a page and hoped-for dreams. While the *SFL Planning* approach focuses on adding these meaningful experiences into your life, it is the monthly, weekly and daily planning processes that will enable you to enjoy those experiences and live your life story.

To facilitate the execution of your *SFL* Plan, it is helpful to have somewhere to record and track your activities at a monthly, weekly, and daily level. The *SFL* concepts can be used with any existing planning system that works for you or any planner of your choice. If you're anything like me, you probably go through planning systems and planners on a regular basis. And there are some good ones out there—simple ones or fancy ones with beautiful covers—you have plenty of choices. I've tried many of them at one point or another. I used many commercially available planners for many years until I finally designed my own to better incorporate the concepts into a formal *SFL Planning System*.

You can find monthly, weekly, and daily planning templates on the SetForLifeExperiences.com website. Having these planning pages, or something similar, will help you as you work through the following steps.

In the previous section, you designed a motivating vision for your life story: You identified your most meaningful roles and the outcomes you deeply desired for those roles, determined the target *SFL Experiences* and finally thought through the *Stepping Stones* that will become part of the overall memory. Now it's time to take the planning to the execution level so you can make that vision happen.

The process below facilitates the linking of shorter-term steps to the longer-term outcomes. An overarching theme to executing your *SFL* Plan is that you will preview what is ahead of you, determine if you are on course, and if not, adjust accordingly. The benefits of the "If-Then" model described earlier apply here as well. The process also ensures the linking between planning horizons. Your monthly, weekly, and daily planning processes are anchored so your *SFL*-related activities don't get lost in some past or future planning horizon.

I agree with the following quote from Bill Gates: "Most people overestimate what they can do in one year and underestimate what they can do in ten years." Similarly, I think we overestimate how much we can do in a day, but underestimate what we can do in a week. We want to approach this process practically and give ourselves a realistic time frame.

The *SFL Planning* process provides you the clarity of knowing your path to achieving your goals from the long-term to the short-term. We plan backward from large to small; we move toward our target *SFL Experience* from the smaller mini-experiences and pre-events that lead us to the larger outcomes.

Think through the following questions as you work through each step. As in the previous section, each step builds on the prior one. The intent is to provide you ideas and a way to think about how you schedule and track the SFL Experiences and Stepping Stones you identified in the previous section.

Nevertheless, if you already have an approach that works for you, keep doing it. The important thing is that you are able to enjoy your *SFL Experiences*.

For the steps below, I use the term *SFL Activities* to mean both SFL Experiences as well as stepping stones.

**Step 5: Monthly Preview**

1. At the beginning of each month preview the *SFL Activities* you planned for the month.
2. Are the *SFL Activities* you scheduled for the month still valid? If yes, are they already scheduled for a specific date? If not, schedule it onto a specific date or a specific future week within the current month in your planner.
3. If the date is no longer valid and the *SFL Activity* will not take place in the current month, reschedule it forward into a future timeframe in your planner. Be as specific as you can be when you are scheduling it into the future (i.e., future month, week, or date).

**Helpful Tips:**

- You can also plan in quarters, i.e., every three months. This type of planning is particularly useful if you like to align your *SFL Planning* to seasons. For example, summer, fall, winter, and spring SFL Activities could be parked within the month that aligns with the three-month quarter.
- Many *SFL Experiences* take place during sports seasons, such as football, basketball, soccer, skiing, etc., or other seasonal activities. You may want to create sports seasons which incorporate *SFL*

*Activities* during those timeframes. This type of seasonal planning keeps things fresh and gives you something to look forward to.
- If you decide to incorporate quarterly or seasonal planning, just preview your *SFL Activities* and Stepping Stones slotted into the quarter and follow the review process, i.e., preview your *SFL Activities* as you enter into a season and follow the monthly review process.
- Regularly review all your *SFL Activities* to make sure they stay top of mind. Life can get busy and we can lose track of what's important. Having a habit of regularly reviewing will enable you to keep the important things in life in front of you.

**Step 6: Weekly Preview**

1. At the beginning of each week (either at the end of the prior week or at the start of a new week), preview any *SFL Activities* planned for the upcoming week.
2. Are the *SFL Activities* you have slotted for the week still valid? If yes, take those that have not been assigned a specific date and schedule them into a particular day in the week.
3. If you are not on track, schedule it forward into a future timeframe in your planner. Be as specific as you can be when you are scheduling it forward (i.e.,

future month, week, or date).

**Helpful Tips:**

- Some people may prefer to plan at the end of the week for the upcoming week to give them a head start. It also may give them a perspective on what can and should be done the upcoming week. Others prefer to do their week's planning at the beginning of the week with the excitement and the motivation of the here and now. Either way, you will have a better view on what your upcoming week's activities look like.
- Take advantage of the weekly preview to identify any loose ends or other things you would like to do and plan them into your week.

**Step 6: Daily Preview**

1. Review your daily schedule each morning or the evening before.
2. Do you have an upcoming *SFL Activity* for that day?
3. If yes, and it's not already scheduled in a time slot, can you schedule the *SFL Activity* during the day?
4. If you are unable to accomplish the *SFL Activity*, reschedule the activity to a future timeframe being as specific as possible (e.g. day/time, week).

**Helpful Tips:**

- Daily schedules and plans are notorious for being changed at the last minute due to unforeseen circumstances and external reasons outside your control. Only you are able to determine whether you can change a scheduled event or whether you need to reschedule. Remember though, sometimes you may have to say no to someone else's request so you can yes to writing YOUR own story.
- A good practice is to schedule the *SFL Activity* like it was an appointment. So, whether it is the monthly, weekly, or daily preview process, when scheduling, try to make it an appointment. This way, you block the time and it's harder to get scheduled over.

As mentioned throughout this book, *SFL Planning* has to work for you. It needs to fit your life for it be useful. While the *SFL Planning* process steps described above are fairly prescriptive, you need to make the process yours. Tailor the process to account for how you live your life. And if you already have a planning system that does work for you, incorporate the *SFL* concepts into what already works to increase your well-being and overall happiness. It's your life. Make it memorable.

# CONCLUSION

*"One lives in the hope of becoming a memory."*

--Antonio Porchia

### FINAL THOUGHTS

Life. When we're young, it stretches out before us almost to eternity. At ten years old, thirty looks ancient. At twenty, it pushes back to forty; that's old to us. As we age, we slide that particular benchmark farther away from our current age because we realize it's all relative. It's something we learn along the way in life. We also learn about context and how that plays a larger role in how happy we are, or what we become...or fail to become.

Often, as we get older, we look for things to make our lives better, more meaningful. We prefer it to be a simple formula—a shortcut, an easy recipe; five minutes to a German chocolate cake that feeds a dozen people; just pressing a button to get instant results. We buy cookbooks that support the latest diet fad because we want quick results. We go for the seven-minute workout, pushing a high-burn regimen into the smallest amount of time possible. That's all good and can work to make select improvements in our lives.

But what we want is the big picture, widescreen high-definition, a life that we dreamed about when we were young. And maybe deep inside we still want this big, colorful life, no matter how old we are. But there is no seven-minute workout for life; there is no quick, easy-bake solution for life; there is no simple formula for life.

Life is about form and substance, and in a figurative sense, it is performance art. Having the life that makes us happy and content can be quantified logically, but it must be orchestrated and choreographed.

Life has become more complex and runs at a faster pace than ever before in history, not just for adults but also for society as a whole. We need to be purposeful in our planning and condition our life to keep happiness and meaning in the forefront of our minds. There are certain types of experiences—*SFL Experiences*, as we've described in this book—that, if we plan them into our lives, can increase our happiness and create a life story worth remembering. And as I've described in this book, these experiences do not have to be expensive. They can be low-cost and even no-cost ways to create moments that truly light up your life and the lives of those around you.

In this book, I reviewed the *SFL Planning* principles and outlined in detail a process that you can follow that will help support the *SFL Planning* approach. The steps and process are straightforward and simple; they do not require sophisticated or complicated planning. At its core is a simple, fundamental rule: Experiences—and memories of them—are what make up our lives, so why not plan to have as many enjoyable experiences as possible to create happy lives? And in a nutshell, that's what this book is about, perhaps more clearly understood by referring to an analogy I've used before: it's how to write the story of your life and fill each chapter with memorable experiences and moments, the kind that make you happy and content. The *SFL* philosophy is about filling our mental scrapbook with the most desirable and pleasurable experiences of our lives, page after page after page.

**Keep Going**

Making or changing a habit is difficult; change is simply very, very hard. Beginning and sustaining the *SFL* approach to planning is the same as making any other change in your life. However, planning this way can increase your happiness and well-being, which is perhaps the single most important goal anyone should have in life.

With an objective like that, why wouldn't someone simply go ahead and make the necessary changes? But again, change is hard; even when we know something is right for us and not that hard to do, people are generally, curiously, resistant to change. We know what we know. The laws of inertia are against us.

Our brains create pathways when we learn how to do something, and doing something repeatedly creates efficiency. After a while, the pathway and associated neurons are well established. In essence, we have learned something new and it becomes *implicit knowledge*. When something new is introduced, those pathways aren't developed. Therefore, doing something new is slow, relatively speaking, and we need to think about what we're doing. But even with the new pathways, we still have the old method of doing something imprinted in our brains, and it has been there far longer than the new way. Therefore, the old way of doing something (the easier and quicker way) and the new, improved way compete with each other. It's a miracle we are able to change at all.

Many other guides and self-help books leave you to figure out how to incorporate into your life what they espouse. You then fight against inertia, the reluctance to change, to keep it going long enough to create that new imprint in your brain. Eventually, the new way finally becomes an implicit memory, one you don't have to consciously think about. Many planning productivity books and systems provide only concepts and ideas; they don't give you the tools to keep them going.

So, in a sense, with these other guides, you are

being set up to fail. But the *SFL Planning System* doesn't just provide you with the concepts and ideas of what you can do to increase your level of happiness—it also gives you the tools, know-how, and a process to follow - the key components needed to sustain a habit. In this way, not only can you apply the fundamental principles to your planning process, but it also gives you the chance to keep them going long enough until they become your own way of doing them; in other words, you build new pathways. While it is laid out in a prescribed manner, you have the opportunity to refine it to meet your own specific and individual needs. *Remember*: The best process is the one you follow, so make it yours.

If you follow what I've shown you about *SFL Planning* and how to use it, you will literally have the experiences of a lifetime. You have one life to live; make it a happy and memorable one.

# REFERENCES

Learn more about the research used in this book in the following resources:

- Why spending money on experiences make people happier than purchasing material goods. In addition, why thinking about experiential purchases has also been shown to produce more positive feelings than thinking about material purchases. Experientialism, Materialism, and the Pursuit of Happiness. Leaf Van Boven University of Colorado at Boulder, 2005.
- Increasing your happiness level can make you healthier and live longer. "Happy People Live Longer: Subjective Well-Being Contributes to Health and Longevity" University of Illinois, Ed Deiner, Micaela Y. Chan, 2011.
- How emotions influence learning and memory processes in the brain. Distinct types of theta rhythmicity are induced by social and fearful stimuli in a network associated with social memory. Dr. Wagner and Ph.D. Alex Tendler, August 2015.
- Why emotional memories - in particular fearful ones, create lasting memories. The fine line between remembering too much and too little.

Memory, the Amygdala, and PTSD. Psychology Today Eyes on the Brain, Posted by Susan R Barry Ph.D. Mar18, 2011.
- The original Princeton University study which suggests your emotional well-being -- or the pleasure you derive from day-to-day experiences -- doesn't get any better after earning a certain amount - which at the time the study was done in 2010 was equal to a household earning roughly $75,000. Princeton University study Daniel Kahneman and Angus Deaton, 2010.
- About the neurotransmitters which affect the way you feel. The Neurochemicals of Happiness. 7 brain molecules that make you feel great. Post published by Christopher Bergland on Nov 29, 2012 in The Athlete's Way.
- The research on experiential purchases and the positive feelings derived from anticipating and from the retelling of those experiences with others. To Do or to Have? That Is the Question. Leaf Van Boven University of Colorado at Boulder Thomas Gilovich Cornell University, 2003.
- "Achieving Sustainable Gains in Happiness: Change Your Actions Not Your Circumstances,"

Journal of Happiness Studies, Sheldon, K. M.; Lyubomirsky, Sonja.
- On how waiting for an experience elicits more excitement than waiting for a material good. Learn why positive feelings start to accrue before an experience. Waiting for Merlot. Anticipatory Consumption of Experiential and Material Purchases. Amit Kumar, Matthew A. Killingsworth, Thomas Gilovich, 2014.
- The study on why physical activity, such as climbing a tree, impacts memory making. Drs. Ross Alloway and Tracy Alloway, University of North Florida, 2015.
- Why experiences that are emotionally arousing are well-remembered and why this mechanism serves to selectively create lasting memories of our more important experiences. Making lasting memories: Remembering the significant, James L. McGaugh, May 9, 2013.
- Statistics on New Year's Resolutions, http://www.statisticbrain.com/new-years-resolution-statistics/
- The value of variety - the spice of life - leads to making happiness last and avoid the hedonic treadmill. The Challenge of Staying Happier Testing the Hedonic Adaptation Prevention Model, Kennon M. Sheldon, Sonja Lyubomirsky, 2014.

- Why we have an innate happiness set point and why we tend to go back there after highs and lows. Hedonic Adaptation to Positive and Negative Experience, Sonja Lyubomirsky, 2011.
- How being in motion makes us happy. Physical Activity and Psychological Well-being, Stuart Biddle, Kenneth R. Fox, Stephen Hugh Boutcher, Psychology Press, 2000.
- How even walking can positively impact our mood. Walking in (Affective) Circles: Can Short Walks Enhance Affect? Panteleimon Ekkekakis,, Eric E. Hall, Lisa M. VanLanduyt, Steven J. Petruzzello, Journal of Behavioral Medicine, June 2000.
- The relative stability of our happiness set point. 1978, Journal of Personality and Social Psychology, Brickman, Philip; Coates, Dan; Janof-BUlman, Ronnie, Northwestern University and the University of Massachusetts, 1978.

# ADDITIONAL RESOURCES

## SFL Planning System Templates

Examples of the forms and templates used can be found at the *Set For Life* website and include Role and Outcome templates, *SFL Experience* and *Stepping Stones* forms and examples of Monthly, Weekly, and Daily Review pages. The link to the site is below.

http://www.SetForLifeExperiences.com

## The Stonecutter (A Japanese Folktale)

This story can be found at Dennis Lowery's website, www.DMLowery.com, by entering the title in the search box and pressing enter or clicking on search. Also, here is a direct link:

http://dmlowery.com/the-stonecutter-a-japanese-folktale-with-afterword-by-dennis-lowery

# ABOUT THE AUTHOR

Ed Elgarresta is a former senior vice president of a Fortune 500 company and a past partner at Accenture. During his 20+ year career of traveling across the country, he learned why the quality of life's experiences matter in creating a happy and memorable life and how to shape and fit what made him most content into a busy schedule.

In a rushed world of too many demands and 'always on' technology-enabled hyper-connectivity, he learned how to look at the quality of his experiences differently and to consciously plan them to make life more enjoyable. The result, simply, was happiness.

Ed wrote *Set For Life* to help other busy people add more joy to their lives. He is dedicated to spreading the message that you can consciously create a remarkable life and how to do it. He and his wife Christina and their two children split their time between homes in Miami, Florida and Philadelphia, Pennsylvania.

www.ingramcontent.com/pod-product-compliance
Lightning Source LLC
Chambersburg PA
CBHW022105040426
42451CB00007B/133